A JOURNEY THROUGH REVELATION

A Journey through Revelation

A Message for the New Millennium

BERTRAND BUBY, SM

ALBA·HOUSE house NEW·YORK

SOCIETY OF ST. PAUL, 2187 VICTORY BLVD., STATEN ISLAND, NEW YORK 10314

ST PAULS

Library of Congress Cataloging-in-Publication Data

Buby, Bertrand.
    A journey through Revelation : a message for the new millennium / Bertrand Buby.
        p. cm.
    Includes bibliographical references.
    ISBN 0-8189-0832-7
    1. Bible. N.T. Revelation—Commentaries. I. Title.

    BS2825.2.B83 2000
    228'.077 — dc21

                                                    99-055451

Produced and designed in the United States of America by the
Fathers and Brothers of the Society of St. Paul,
2187 Victory Boulevard, Staten Island, New York 10314-6603,
as part of their communications apostolate.

ISBN: 0-8189-0832-7

Printing Information:

Current Printing - first digit   1   2   3   4   5   6   7   8   9   10

Year of Current Printing - first year shown

2000   2001   2002   2003   2004   2005   2006   2007   2008   2009

ACKNOWLEDGMENTS

Through the assistance and creative insights of the following persons, I was able to complete this spiritual journey through Revelation:

Eileen Cehyra, FMI: in appreciation for her long hours in preparing and revising the text.

Eileen Moorman: who clarified and polished the work for a reader friendly audience.

Connie Breen: who offered encouragement and support along the way.

Gene Contadino, SM, Gerald Chinchar, SM, and Jean Frisk, a Schoenstatt Sister: who assisted with the technical dimension of this project.

TABLE OF CONTENTS

PREFACE

After having read and researched Revelation both from ancient writings and up-to-date commentaries, I decided to write my own reflections on this difficult, enigmatic, and symbolic book. I, personally, became interested in its meaning and message during the Easter season when it is used for the Office of Readings. I wondered why it was chosen for this season. I noticed that Revelation is one of the most cited sections of Scripture used in the liturgical hours of the Church; as a hymn, as a response, and as a parenthetical hint at what the psalms or readings are about. This led me to be attentive to the revelatory message of this final writing in the New Testament (that is, canonically placed at the end though not chronologically the last).

With the new millennium I knew that Revelation would be a sensationally popular book of the Bible. It would be studied and carefully researched in the academies of biblical studies; it would be popularized by charismatic preachers and teachers; it would also be taken up in the newspapers, the movies and the Internet. I found myself interested and excited about exploring all of these opportunities for learning about this apocalyptic work.

However, it was the spirituality of God's Word that led me to enjoy reading it, meditating on its chapters, and researching it, so to speak, from beginning to end. The more I read and meditated on its pages, the more I felt energized and challenged to discover its spiritual, theological, and ethical meanings. After researching it carefully, I realized that all of these ways and methods of understanding it were somewhat like the Book of Revelation itself. They blend into one another and help one to listen and retell the story from so many new, interesting, and profitable ways.

To retell the story in a new way is a challenge, for much ink and print has been given to this tantalizing tale. I was left with the impression that it was only the areas of spirituality and biblical theology which were not overly developed by contemporary students and scholars. The medieval and earliest writers were interested in and developed its theology, but often in a limited manner. They were bound by their times and cultures. Often a monastic application, or during and after the Reformation, a polemic use of Revelation was developed.

My own personal interest continued to grow and, as I approached the task of writing, I realized that I was focusing more and more on its theological and spiritual purposes. I believe that the revelatory message of the book is where God breaks through all of the worlds of the text. This requires the writer, reader, and student of the text to have the grace and gift of faith to see and understand the essential and core value of the book of Revelation. This Word demands both study — reflective and meditative — as well as pondering over it as the Mother of Jesus did in Luke's Infancy narrative (Lk 2:19,51). The words then become an event, a happening, a moment of communication with God. Somehow this occurs when one opens oneself to God's word with a listening heart as well as an inquisitive and enlightened mind. In addition, a passionate desire should not be missing from this endeavor.

To prepare myself for this new look at Revelation I began reading the Greek text over and over again. I returned to the English translations easily available to me (R.S.V., N.R.S.V. Jerusalem, New American, K.J., etc.) and then returned again to the Greek. I also used a Hebrew translation (Delitsch) in order to catch the Semitic flavor that undoubtedly permeates this book. As a follow-up I began to look at the vocabulary used by the author to see where else such words are used in the New Testament. The task seemed endless but, the more I took it up, the greater my passion for this book grew.

The work of every scholar rests on the shoulders of the giants of the past whether they be somewhat contemporary or whether they are those from the first millennium. Each person who reasonably and reverently approaches the book comes away with various insights and facets of the truth. The picture puzzle of Revelation has only its framework completed. What is being researched and discovered are important pieces which fit together inside that framework. And, yet, such an image does not suffice. It is as though these pieces are within the framework of a kaleidoscope that gradually reveals magnificent patterns and colors so reflective of the symbolism and plasticity of Revelation.

Since I am already at the age of Kronus, I am less afraid to approach this amazing book from a faith-inspired and theological method — a God-centered method. I, however, am assured that it is possible to do this type of a reflection only after having carefully studied the major commentators and the contemporary experts who make this book come alive in so many new and exciting ways. I will mention these important scholars and their works as I move through these pages.

In most recent writings about the Book of Revelation, the art of narrative has supplied readers with knowing how important a story is. Today the story of Revelation is being told and analyzed by these marvelous students of literary criticism. Such an art and science, for that matter, enable other students to reflect and learn much from this book. As a person of prayer and one engaged in spiritual direction, I have learned how to interpret better the book of Revelation because of these recent authors and their publications. Theology and spirituality are moderated and framed by such responsible works.

> "Behold I (Jesus) stand at the door and I am knocking; if you happen to hear my voice and then open the door, I will sit down with you and you with me. To the victorious I will grant a place with me on my throne, even as I have been victorious and have sat down with my God upon the throne. You who have ears, listen to what the Spirit is saying to the churches" (Rv 3:20-22).
> [Interpretative translation of author]

INTRODUCTION

Several years ago I was struck by the readings offered in the prayer of the Church during the Easter Season. This continuous reading of Revelation during the Easter cycle made me ponder over its message and its points of view. I came to realize that it has a simple but important call: "Worship God."

In reflecting upon it further, I saw that the image of Jesus as the Passover Lamb is a central symbol for the Lord who, in his words, "always sits at the right hand of God."

The message of Revelation is a celebration of the victory of Jesus Christ over death, sin, and evil. Jesus united heaven and earth through his death on the Cross. This belief in the union of all believers with him is known as the "Communion of Saints." People from the past, the present, and the future are called to be a community of believers who worship no one but God the Father and the victorious Lamb, Jesus Christ, through the Holy Spirit. Priorities are put in order once the pilgrim Christian understands this commandment of Revelation.

These thoughts and beliefs led me to study and research in depth the book of Revelation. I became impassioned about this task and started to gather commentaries on it, selecting the very best. I was lead to research the earliest treatises done by the theologians of the first centuries, next the Middle Ages, and especially the contemporary works of exegetes, theologians, and spiritual writers. The research became a journey which led me to retrace, and, so to speak, attempt to walk in the sandals of John of Patmos, the prophet and mystic seer of the book of Revelation.

After two years of serious study and note taking, I decided to write about my journey through Revelation in a reader friendly way.

This resulted in the layout I use in this commentary. To make Revelation palatable for readers, I constructed my interpretation and spiritual reflections with a threefold presentation based on the established text of the narrative of John of Patmos.

The revealed text is the most important foundation for every exegete, theologian, and pastor. This gift to us is the primary source or witness of an experience that John of Patmos (the name many exegetes give to the prophet) had on the Lord's day, that is, on Sunday, while desiring to celebrate the Eucharist with one of the seven churches in Asia Minor.

Since I had studied, listened, and read the original Koine Greek text about thirty or more times — often listening to the entire text in one sitting, I began to think about "walking in the sandals" of John. This led me to develop short soliloquies in which I attempt to share with you the mind and heart of the visionary. I think I was led to this first step of the journey by hearing my own recorded voice reading the Greek text of Revelation while pondering over its messages. I did this after morning prayer each day during the past two and a half years. Soon I became familiar with key words, simple phrases, and the theology behind the work. I realized how John himself pondered over the Hebrew Scriptures and alluded to them hundreds of times in his 22 chapters.

After having composed a retelling of John's vision in chapter one, I shared it with several congregations and with some scholars. One scholar advised me to do the same at given and fixed intervals. This would help the reader to enter into the world of the author, John of Patmos. Hence, the first journey in the footsteps of the seer, assists the reader through the first chapter. One walks with John of Patmos through his soliloquy.

The second stage of the journey is more the result of interpretation, personal yet moderated by the commentaries of the best exegetes who have given us the social location of the work, its literary complexities, and its careful philological make-up.

For this task, I used the method known as the "Worlds of the Text" to analyze exegetical works. I asked one of the readers to make sure I did not overstep my boundaries by going beyond what actually was within the text and behind the text.

Finally, in my other readings and reflective moments, I began to select passages outside of Revelation which helped me to understand and experience what the text was saying to me. This is the third reader friendly aid for the journey through Revelation. I named it "Food for the Journey."

My purpose in writing this book is to help others appreciate God's multiple ways of revelation in the Bible. God uses human language to communicate with us in these texts. The book of Revelation is not different from the other modes of revelation except in its rich imagery and symbolism. I also wanted to assure readers that this book is helpful for those who will read it in the third millennium. This book is not to be feared for it is a work of hope and freedom. For our role as readers, John would have us professing our faith in the Word of God as well as in the testimony or witness that we give to Jesus through his Passion, Death, and Resurrection. In addition to our fidelity and trust in God's Word there is a special virtue the visionary would have us possess — "patient endurance." In Greek the word is *hypomene*. It can be interpreted as consistent resistance to the false values of any "-ism" but perhaps especially secularism. J.B. Phillips translated this word *hypomene* as "sheer dogged endurance." May I offer one last understanding of the word? I would suggest the simple word "patience" — a virtue that overcomes fear, avoids rash judgments, and moderates the desire to have a "quick fix."

Finally as a prayer found in Revelation I suggest a few of its own special liturgical phrases: "Amen!," "Alleluia!" and "Come, Lord Jesus" (*Maranatha*)!

Biblical Abbreviations

OLD TESTAMENT

Genesis	Gn	Nehemiah	Ne	Baruch	Ba
Exodus	Ex	Tobit	Tb	Ezekiel	Ezk
Leviticus	Lv	Judith	Jdt	Daniel	Dn
Numbers	Nb	Esther	Est	Hosea	Ho
Deuteronomy	Dt	1 Maccabees	1 M	Joel	Jl
Joshua	Jos	2 Maccabees	2 M	Amos	Am
Judges	Jg	Job	Jb	Obadiah	Ob
Ruth	Rt	Psalms	Ps	Jonah	Jon
1 Samuel	1 S	Proverbs	Pr	Micah	Mi
2 Samuel	2 S	Ecclesiastes	Ec	Nahum	Na
1 Kings	1 K	Song of Songs	Sg	Habakkuk	Hab
2 Kings	2 K	Wisdom	Ws	Zephaniah	Zp
1 Chronicles	1 Ch	Sirach	Si	Haggai	Hg
2 Chronicles	2 Ch	Isaiah	Is	Malachi	Ml
Ezra	Ezr	Jeremiah	Jr	Zechariah	Zc
		Lamentations	Lm		

NEW TESTAMENT

Matthew	Mt	Ephesians	Eph	Hebrews	Heb
Mark	Mk	Philippians	Ph	James	Jm
Luke	Lk	Colossians	Col	1 Peter	1 P
John	Jn	1 Thessalonians	1 Th	2 Peter	2 P
Acts	Ac	2 Thessalonians	2 Th	1 John	1 Jn
Romans	Rm	1 Timothy	1 Tm	2 John	2 Jn
1 Corinthians	1 Cor	2 Timothy	2 Tm	3 John	3 Jn
2 Corinthians	2 Cor	Titus	Tt	Jude	Jude
Galatians	Gal	Philemon	Phm	Revelation	Rv

A JOURNEY THROUGH REVELATION

Chapter One

JESUS REVEALS HIMSELF TO JOHN OF PATMOS
(Rv 1:1-20)

Revelation 1:1-20

¹The revelation of Jesus Christ, which God gave him to show his servants what must soon take place; he made it known by sending his angel to his servant John, ²who testified to the word of God and to the testimony of Jesus Christ, even to all that he saw. ³Blessed is the one who reads aloud the words of the prophecy, and blessed are those who hear and who keep what is written in it; for the time is near.

⁴John to the seven churches that are in Asia: Grace to you and peace from him who is and who was and who is to come, and from the seven spirits who are before his throne, ⁵and from Jesus Christ, the faithful witness, the firstborn of the dead, and the ruler of the kings of the earth. To him who loves us and freed us from our sins by his blood, ⁶and made us to be a kingdom, priests serving his God and Father, to him be glory and dominion forever and ever. Amen. ⁷Look! He is coming with the clouds; every eye will see him, even those who pierced him; and on his account all the tribes of the earth will wail. So it is to be. Amen. ⁸"I am the Alpha and the Omega,' says the Lord God, who is and who was and who is to come, the Almighty.

⁹I, John, your brother who share with you in Jesus the persecution and the kingdom and the patient endurance, was on the

1

island called Patmos because of the word of God and the testimony of Jesus. [10]I was in the spirit on the Lord's day, and I heard behind me a loud voice like a trumpet [11]saying, "Write in a book what you see and send it to the seven churches, to Ephesus, to Smyrna, to Pergamum, to Thyatira, to Sardis, to Philadelphia, and to Laodicea." [12]Then I turned to see whose voice it was that spoke to me, and on turning I saw seven golden lampstands, [13]and in the midst of the lampstands I saw one like the Son of Man, clothed with a long robe and with a golden sash across his chest. [14]His head and his hair were white as white wool, white as snow; his eyes were like a flame of fire, [15]his feet were like burnished bronze, refined as in a furnace, and his voice was like the sound of many waters. [16]In his right hand he held seven stars, and from his mouth came a sharp, two-edged sword, and his face was like the sun shining with full force.

[17]When I saw him, I fell at his feet as though dead. But he placed his right hand on me, saying, "Do not be afraid; I am the first and the last, [18]and the living one. I was dead, and see, I am alive forever and ever; and I have the keys of Death and of Hades. [19]Now write what you have seen, what is, and what is to take place after this. [20]As for the mystery of the seven stars that you saw in my right hand, and the seven golden lampstands: the seven stars are the angels of the seven churches, and the seven lampstands are the seven churches.

COMMENTARY

Revelation 1

John of Patmos is the name the author of Revelation has given us for this apocalyptic masterpiece of the New Testament. John, like other inspired servants of God, gives us a comprehensive introduction to the unfolding of the drama which will unravel in three overlapping scenes. Introductions are often keys to understanding the motifs, themes, and intention of the writer, prophet, or visionary. In our particular book, John of Patmos is prophet, writer, and visionary.

His background displays familiarity with the first testament, the Hebrew scriptures. Every scholar who has examined his work realizes how often the visionary alludes to the prophetic literature and the only authentic apocalyptic work of the inspired scriptures of Judaism, to wit, the book of Daniel. Some scholars think there may be as many as two hundred oblique allusions to the first testament. Some even imagine that every line of Revelation contains a hint of the Jewish inspired heritage. For the reader, this is helpful information for interpreting this symbolic writing. Cross-references and parallel passages are basic to a correct exegesis of the biblical library of both testaments.

Like most interpreters, I would find John of Patmos to be a Jewish Christian of the first century who recalls his experiences with God from a period of his life that embraces the present (somewhere during Domitian's reign in Rome 81-96 C.E.) with his past which may have anteceded the rule of the maniac emperor, Nero (54-68 C.E.).

In reconstructing the experience of John of Patmos as portrayed in his first Chapter (Rv 1:1-19), I put myself in the sandals of John allowing him, through my imagination, to tell us about his initial experience and call to be a visionary and a Christian prophet.

John of Patmos speaks:

It all happened on the Lord's Day, or what you would call a Sunday. On this day, we Christians celebrate the Resurrection of Jesus in the reenactment of the Lord's Supper, the Eucharist. I, John, am a convert from Judaism to Christianity. I am three generations removed from the death of Jesus in the holy city of Jerusalem. I am not the apostle John, the son of Zebedee. I was in a cave on the island of Patmos and was longing to be with my fellow Christian sisters and brothers in Ephesus just across the Aegean Sea some forty to fifty miles away. The Romans sent me here to this wretched confinement. They control everything these days and are influencing many Christians to take on their culture, language, and beliefs. They are attractive to us for they have so much to offer in this crazy world of ours — merchandise, weapons, jewelry, cosmetics. You name it! They have it! There are twenty-four hours of tantalizing commercials with all sorts of sensuous temptations, many of which start at the large bathhouses in our coastal cities, like Ephesus. Some of these Christians at Ephesus are so enamored by the Romans that they are even buying food that has been offered to the Roman deities. How base can we get? And here I am confined to this wretched island without any possibility of celebrating the Lord's Supper this Resurrection Day.

Then suddenly it happened. I was struck by a brilliant light from the sky and I heard powerful voices and the roar of many waves against the non-too-distant shore. My cave reverberates with all sorts of noises from the outside. Only this time it was very terrifying. Yet, at once I was calmed for I was listening to the most beautiful voice I have ever heard telling me that I had to contact the Christian Churches in the Roman Province of Asia: Ephesus, Smyrna, Pergamum, Thyatira, Sardis, Philadelphia, and Laodicea. Then the brilliance of the one speaking awakened all my senses. I was convinced it could only be my Lord Jesus who was directly speaking to me. In fact, it was a revelation — an apocalypse — an opening up of many events to come and some of which already had happened. I was caught up in this ecstatic wonderment of sight and sound. Jesus had come to me on this Sunday and now, I was, in a sense, sharing in the Lord's Eucharist — the Lord's Resurrection — and the fullness of his presence in the remembering of the Last Supper.

It became very clear to me that Jesus was calling me to assume a prophetic role and to be a preacher to the seven churches I had often visited and served, making the rounds as his devoted disciple and servant.

The vision continued and I became aware that I was neither in time nor space. Jesus was speaking as the Eternal Word, the beginning and the end, the Alpha and the Omega. Then another voice resounded from behind me and it was a messenger of God and Jesus — an angel. Suddenly I started to remember the Scriptures — all of them — the Torah, the Prophets, and the Psalms. The angel seemed to be spilling all of these beautiful words and writings into my head, my eyes, my ears, and my heart. I now knew what they meant and how Jesus had fulfilled them not so long ago in that Holy Land of Galilee and Judea.

It was crystal clear that all of us were washed and freed from our sins because of the Lamb of God, slain on Calvary, on the life-giving Roman instrument of execution, the Cross. Now he was truly alive, the victorious Lamb of God, the Lion of Juda, the Root of David. He was the resurrected Son of Man and the Alpha and Omega of all creation. And the vision kept on; I felt the urge to crawl back into the hollow depth of my cell, the cave. But the voices were so compelling — both that of Jesus and that of the angel. I was told not to be afraid. I was somehow to write about this experience in three scrolls and share the revelation with the seven churches through someone who would read them in front of my brothers and sisters. This vision was timeless, yet, there were unfolding successive scenes and many symbols that enlightened me about the Scriptures as well as what I knew from what had been handed down to me by the followers of the apostles.

Suddenly scrolls seemed to pop up in front of me: three of them. I began to write furiously and quickly. I had been a well-trained scribe to begin with. I wrote what I heard, saw, and experienced. Call it a theophany or an ecstasy; call it a foreseeing, a remembering. It was all of these blended and bound up in the marvelous revelation of Jesus Christ. It was a true apocalypse.

My writing seemed to move swiftly onto the scrolls, first, the one addressed to the churches; then the second, my experience of what it means to be in the presence of the living God, what it means to really worship God; and finally, the third scroll, the scroll of crisis, catharsis, and conflict. I remembered the Dead Sea Community and how it had constructed similar scrolls: a Rule for the Community, a Temple Scroll, and a War Scroll. But this was different. I was experiencing what I wrote about. It was revelatory, real, and tremendous. It all happened in the twinkle of an eye and yet it perdured, as it were, forever.

COMMENTARY

Revelation 1:1-3

Jesus Christ is the revealing and revelatory hero of the symbolic narrative that unfolds in twenty-two chapters. The first word "Apocalypse" is best translated as revelation. Thus this book of the New Testament is given its name from the introductory word. Both "Apocalypse" and "Revelation" are used for naming the book; the more traditional one being Apocalypse. The basic meaning behind the verb is "to reveal something that previously has been hidden." Jesus is the Revealer in this inspired writing and also within the Johannine tradition as contrasted with the Synoptics.

The recipient of the revelation is John of Patmos who is not the apostle John. This person who gives us his name as John is usually understood to be a Palestinian Jewish convert to Christianity. He has been exiled to the island of Patmos, a small island to the west of Ephesus in Asia Minor (present day Turkey).

The message is conveyed through an angel or messenger who speaks to the servant of Jesus (a follower and believer) who has witnessed to the word of God and to the person of Jesus. This message is to be shared with other servants of God (Christians in the seven churches of Asia Minor) for it concerns things or events that soon must happen. The one who announces this and those who listen with open hearts are called blessed or fortunate for the prophecy they are about to hear is urgent and compelling. The author will use the word blessed or fortunate seven times throughout Revelation. In scriptural terms these are equivalent to seven beatitudes, differing, of course, from the traditional listing of beatitudes in Matthew 5:1-11 and Luke 6:20-23.

E. Corsini, in his unique and creative interpretation of Revelation, considers the angel or messenger as one who speaks to John about the prophetic messages of the Hebrew scriptures. The chief works alluded to are Daniel, Ezekiel, Isaiah, and Zechariah.

In verse 1 the expression "what must take place soon" is emphasized after the beatitude with a more precise phrase, "for the opportune time is near." Our visionary author has a unique style of knitting ideas together with his choice of words.

The Epistolary Salutation

Verses 4 through 6 are the prescript of the letter which John of Patmos wishes to address to the seven churches. It is the message from the Revealer Jesus and also from the messenger of God, an angel who discloses the prophetic words of the scriptures to the recipient who in turn will allude to them throughout his visionary experience.

John of Patmos is the sender. He greets the seven churches with the characteristic grace and peace of the epistles of the New Testament. The content, however, is coming from the "one who is, who was and who is coming," and also from the holy seven spirits who represent the churches before the throne of God. We could name them the guardians or angels of these churches. However, it is the Revealer himself — Jesus, who is the faithful witness and the first born to rise from the dead, victorious over death and sin. He is the true leader of all kings upon the earth.

Unlike the author of the Fourth Gospel, this John of Patmos emphasizes the fact that those who are addressed have been freed or washed by the blood of Jesus thereby sharing in the priesthood and kingdom of Jesus and of God. Reverently, the author ends the address (verse 6) with a doxology or prayer of praise: "to him be glory and dominion forever. Amen." These exclamations of praise of God in this Hebrew formulation are presented throughout the entire book of Revelation. This reminds us that our writer is a Jewish Christian who is at ease with prayers of praise and with the prophets.

Two Prophetic Sayings (1:7-8)

The first prophet to be cited by our author is Daniel 7:13 in a text that refers to the coming of a human figure upon the clouds. This text has been applied to Jesus in the synoptics (Mt 24:30; Mk 13:36; Lk 21:27). The other favored prophet is Zechariah 12:10 "every eye will see him, even those who pierced him." In John's Gospel we find the same text being used to describe Jesus' death upon the cross.

Once again the visionary ends these prophetic sayings with a prayerful, Yes! so be it — an Amen!

Verse 8 is an *ego eimi* (I am) statement coming from the Lord who declares himself to be the Alpha and the Omega. These two letters of the Greek alphabet are the first and last thus symbolizing Jesus, the Lord, as the beginning and end of all God's creation. Again it is knitted to what has gone before, namely, to the one who is, who was and who is coming, the *Pantocrator* or Almighty One.

Most probably, the last line applies to God, but as Revelation unfolds, we also realize it can be speaking of the supreme Revealer of God, the Lord Jesus Christ whom the Eastern tradition calls *Pantocrator* (Rv 1:8).

The Vision and Manifestation of Christ to John of Patmos (1:9-20)

Isolated on Patmos, the prophetic witness John reminds the listening or reading believers that he has patiently endured being separated from the churches of which he is so fond. He relates to them his experience on a Sunday, the Lord's day. The clarion voice of God's messenger tells him to write on a scroll what he now is about to see. The churches, which are not distant from each other, are to be informed. Perhaps he had visited and spoken to them several times before his exile to Patmos. Now he is called to write to them at Ephesus, Smyrna, Pergamum, Thyatira, Sardis, Philadelphia, and Laodicea. The Lord's day commemorates the Resurrection of Jesus. Here in Rv 1:10, we have the first direct attestation to such a remembrance on a Sunday.

The Son of Man stands among the seven lampstands which represent the seven churches. Jesus, the Risen One, calms John just as he had calmed his terrified disciples on the Lake of Galilee by placing his hand upon him while saying, "Do not be afraid; I am the first and the last, and the living one. I was dead, and see, I am alive forever and ever." Though not celebrating the Lord's Day with the seven churches, John of Patmos is experiencing through this epiphany what the churches would be celebrating liturgically in the reading of the Scriptures and in the Eucharist.

Verses 10 through 20 are simply the command to write about this vision. Several of the symbols are directly interpreted which helps the reader and listener to understand the meaning of the seven golden lampstands. They represent the seven churches while the seven stars of the scene are the guardian angels of the churches. All is held together by the Lord, the *Pantocrator*.

Food for the Journey:

Daniel 7:9-13

⁹As I watched, thrones were set in place, and an Ancient One took his throne, his clothing was white as snow, and the hair of his head like pure wool; his throne was fiery flames, and its wheels were burning fire. ¹⁰A stream of fire issued and flowed out from his presence. A thousand thousands served him, and ten thousand times ten thousand stood attending him. The court sat in judgment, and the books were opened. ¹¹I watched then because of the noise of the arrogant words that the horn was speaking. And as I watched, the beast was put to death, and its body destroyed and given over to be burned with fire. ¹²As for the rest of the beasts, their dominion was taken away, but their lives were prolonged for a season and a time. ¹³As I watched in the night visions, I saw

one like a human being coming with the clouds of heaven. And he came to the Ancient One and was presented before him.

Exodus 3:13-15

[13]But Moses said to God, "If I come to the Israelites and say to them, 'The God of your ancestors has sent me to you,' and they ask me, 'What is his name?' what shall I say to them?" [14]God said to Moses, "I Am Who I Am." He said further, "Thus you shall say to the Israelites, 'I Am has sent me to you.'" [15]God also said to Moses, "Thus you shall say to the Israelites, 'The Lord, the God of your ancestors, the God of Abraham, the God of Isaac, and the God of Jacob, has sent me to you': This is my name forever, and this my title for all generations."

CHAPTER TWO

JOHN OF PATMOS ADDRESSES
THE SEVEN CHURCHES
(Rv 2-3)

Revelation 2:1-29

[1]"To the angel of the church in Ephesus write: 'These are the words of him who holds the seven stars in his right hand, who walks among the seven golden lampstands: [2]"I know your works, your toil and your patient endurance. I know that you cannot tolerate evildoers; you have tested those who claim to be apostles but are not, and have found them to be false. [3]I also know that you are enduring patiently and bearing up for the sake of my name, and that you have not grown weary. [4]But I have this against you, that you have abandoned the love you had at first. [5]Remember then from what you have fallen; repent, and do the works you did at first. If not, I will come to you and remove your lampstand from its place, unless you repent. [6]Yet this is to your credit: you hate the works of the Nicolaitans, which I also hate. [7]Let anyone who has an ear listen to what the Spirit is saying to the churches. To everyone who conquers, I will give permission to eat from the tree of life that is in the paradise of God."

[8]"And to the angel of the church in Smyrna write: 'These are the words of the first and the last, who was dead and came to life: [9]"I know your affliction and your poverty, even though you are rich. I know the slander on the part of those who say that they are Jews and are not, but are a synagogue of Satan. [10]Do not fear

11

what you are about to suffer. Beware, the devil is about to throw some of you into prison so that you may be tested, and for ten days you will have affliction. Be faithful until death, and I will give you the crown of life. [11]Let anyone who has an ear listen to what the Spirit is saying to the churches. Whoever conquers will not be harmed by the second death."

[12]"And to the angel of the church in Pergamum write: 'These are the words of him who has the sharp two-edged sword: [13]"I know where you are living, where Satan's throne is. Yet you are holding fast to my name, and you did not deny your faith in me even in the days of Antipas my witness, my faithful one, who was killed among you, where Satan lives. [14]But I have a few things against you: you have some there who hold to the teaching of Balaam, who taught Balak to put a stumbling block before the people of Israel, so that they would eat food sacrificed to idols and practice fornication. [15]So you also have some who hold to the teaching of the Nicolaitans. [16]Repent then. If not, I will come to you soon and make war against them with the sword of my mouth. [17]Let anyone who has an ear listen to what the Spirit is saying to the churches. To everyone who conquers I will give some of the hidden manna, and I will give a white stone, and on the white stone is written a new name that no one knows except the one who receives it."

[18]"And to the angel of the church in Thyatira write: 'These are the words of the Son of God, who has eyes like a flame of fire, and whose feet are like burnished bronze: [19]"I know your works — your love, faith, service, and patient endurance. I know that your last works are greater than the first. [20]But I have this against you: you tolerate that woman Jezebel, who calls herself a prophet and is teaching and beguiling my servants to practice fornication and to eat food sacrificed to idols. [21]I gave her time to repent, but she refuses to repent of her fornication. [22]Beware, I am throwing her on a bed, and those who commit adultery with her I am throwing into great distress, unless they repent of her doings; [23]and I will strike her children dead. And all the churches will know that I am the one who searches minds and hearts, and I will give to each of you as your works deserve. [24]But to the rest of you in

Thyatira, who do not hold this teaching, who have not learned what some call 'the deep things of Satan,' to you I say, I do not lay on you any other burden; [25]only hold fast to what you have until I come. [26]To everyone who conquers and continues to do my works to the end, I will give authority over the nations; [27]to rule them with an iron rod, as when clay pots are shattered — [28]even as I also received authority from my Father. To the one who conquers I will also give the morning star. [29]Let anyone who has an ear listen to what the Spirit is saying to the churches.'"

John of Patmos speaks:

I, John of Patmos, then heard a voice like a loud trumpet summoning me to write letters to the seven churches I had often visited in the Province of Asia. These seven different messages were to be written within a large scroll and then read to each church congregation. They would then know how they were being assessed by God. I was to be the prophet and the scribe for these revelations. Know that these messages will help you to understand the entire experience that I am going to tell you. The information I already knew through my own travels to these house churches, as well as the revelation coming from the angelic voice will help you to read more accurately the entire apocalypse. I fear that future Christians like yourself may misinterpret the content of the letters which only applies to my lifetime and my experiences. The symbolism I use is that of the era in which I live.

The individual letters have the same pattern, but, look carefully for some differences. For example, I was to write good things about the church in Smyrna and Philadelphia whereas for Sardis and Laodicea, there are no compliments from the revealer.

The primary concerns of the letters are false teaching (Ephesus, Pergamum, Thyatira), persecution in Smyrna and Philadelphia, and finally complacency in Sardis and Laodicea. I exhort those who are reading these letters to pay more attention to the issue of complacency. I am convinced that people are easily led by their own cultural biases and false values. Reading the signs of the times does not mean giving in to the political powers and situational ethics that tend to influence us in the present generation.

I was, at first, apprehensive about writing to the churches, but the angel's voice was so articulate and convincing that I wrote as a skillful scribe. The Lord Jesus was to be mentioned in each address, then the status of the churches that I already knew; finally some admonitions and encouragement were to be given with a call to listen carefully to what the Spirit was saying to each church.

COMMENTARY

The Seer Addresses the Seven Churches

The seer now addresses the seven churches in Western Asia Minor in the following order: Ephesus, Smyrna, Pergamum, Thyatira, Sardis, Philadelphia, and Laodicea. These cities of the Roman province of Asia are located within a radius of 150 miles. Pergamum is the northern most city, Laodicea the southeastern most, while Ephesus is the first to be mentioned and is on the western coastline. Patmos on the Aegean Sea is southeast of Ephesus also within 150 miles. Our visionary may have been an itinerant missionary who was familiar with all seven churches. His message to each is patterned along the same lines, but developed according to the situation and ethical behavior of each community. The pattern of these letters makes an easy read for us. The structure consists in: (1) giving titles to Christ (Christology) that have already been announced in chapter one. Jesus is seen, for example, as the one holding seven stars and walking among the lampstands (Ephesus: Rv 2:1). Each church will be addressed by Christ who has a different title. (2) The church is then evaluated as either doing good things or as not living up to Christian ideals. (3) The call to conversion (*metanoia*), if needed, or encouragement for living out its ideals then follows. (4) A special promise is given to those churches who are victorious over the evils which they experience.

The Church at Ephesus (Rv 2:1-7)

Ephesus. This is a city in Lydia (today it is called Keciek Mendere) at the mouth of the Kazstei River. It always had been known as the capital city of the Province of Asia even up to the reign of Diocletian (284-305 C.E.). This city flourished as a religious center, had an academy of medicine (the Mouseion) and housed the famous library of Celsus. It was considered to be the second home of John, the beloved disciple, and Mary the Mother of Jesus. The words of the one holding the seven stars in his hand amidst the seven lampstands, praises the church at Ephesus for its patient endurance and for its testing those who claim to be apostles but are not. Jesus calls Ephesus to return to its original commitment of love and the words of love, otherwise its lampstand (the existence and authority of the church) will be removed. However, the Nicolaitans are not tolerated; the Lord commends Ephesus for doing this.

Who were the Nicolaitans also mentioned in the references to the church at Smyrna (50 miles north of Ephesus)? They probably belonged to a sect which emphasized certain doctrines and morals contrary to that held by Jews and Christians. Perhaps they were charlatans and self-proclaimed itinerant preachers who bothered the churches (Rv 2:6,14,16,20). They had no scruples about partaking in pagan banquets where food was offered to idols or in the name of the emperor. Were they possibly associated with the deacon mentioned in Acts 6:5 known as Nicolaus? It seems they may have been involved in immoral practices since the names Balaam and Jezebel are mentioned in the scroll to the churches (Rv 2:14,19). Both led the people of Israel to idolatrous practices. Whoever they are, they are self-proclaimed prophets seeking to seduce the communities of Christians. Perhaps, a type of pregnostic laxism and libertinism was their selling point. The nearby bathhouses of Ephesus would provide a platform for them as well as the churches and synagogues. The words used in Revelation about them are couched in symbolic language and connect idolatrous worship with sexual immorality such as fornication. The call to the perfection of love (agape) would be just the opposite to what the Nicolaitans were promoting.

The final words to the church at Ephesus are a call to be attentive to the Spirit. Such discernment of the spirits would lead the community to eat and partake of the tree of life in God's original plan rather than at secular banquets. Harkening back to Genesis 2:8 and the Garden of Eden, the Ephesians are promised an opportunity to eat from the tree of life in the Paradise of God. They would enjoy a form of eternal life through their attentiveness to God and their original commitment of love.

The Church at Smyrna (Rv 2:8-10)

Smyrna, today's Izmir, is a port city in western Turkey. It is within 40 miles from Ephesus to the north. This city was dedicated to the imperial cult. In its history Smyrna was a bitter rival of Ephesus. Homer is associated with Smyrna. This city had beautiful buildings, especially its temples. The emperors Augustus and Tiberius were influential in fostering the imperial cult in this city. We have to keep in mind that the book of Revelation is directly confronting the power, cult, and immorality of the Roman Empire. Only God is to be worshiped. This is the top priority of Revelation which can be summed up in the phrase "Worship God!" Smyrna is mentioned twice in Revelation (1:11 and here in 2:8). Later Polycarp would be the bishop of Smyrna. There also was a Jewish population in this city as seen by the reference to the Jews and the synagogue. Archaeological studies attest to the fact that Jews and Christians set up booths for vending side by side. In times of more intense imperial worship there is the possibility that some Jews may have turned in the names of Christians to the authorities. Modern scholarly opinion holds that there was no serious persecution in Asia Minor during the time in which Revelation was written. This opinion is gaining ground over the commonly accepted idea that Christians were severely punished by the Romans between the reign of Nero and Domitian (54-96 C.E.).

Christ, in addressing the community at Smyrna is described as "the first and the last, who was dead and came to life." This description has already been announced in Revelation 1:5,8. The community is probably being slandered by some Jews from the synagogue. These Christians are materially poor, but spiritually rich. The speaker tells them to fear neither suffering nor being thrown into prison. Perseverance is encouraged; there is nothing bad said about them in their situation. They are promised a crown or wreath of life (spiritual immortality as a reward). The refrain about listening to the Spirit is continuous for all seven churches. The tribulation this community is experiencing is described by David Aune, today's foremost scholar and exegete of Revelation: "This community, which apparently had few if any wealthy members (v. 9), had experienced severe persecution as the apparent result of Jewish slander. They are not *real* Jews, claims John, but a synagogue of Satan. This implies that Christians are the true Israel (a widespread Christian view; cf. Jn 4:23-24; Gal 6:16; Phil 3:3; 1 P 2:9-10; Barnabus 4:6-7; Justin Dialogue 11:5) and that unconverted Jews are outside the people of God" (Aune, D., Revelation. *Word Biblical Commentary 52A*, pp. 175-176).

The Church at Pergamum (Rv 2:12-17)

Pergamum (now Bergama) is located 16 miles inland from the Aegean Sea and is 70 miles north of Smyrna. This city came into prominence after Alexander the Great (333 B.C.E.). R.E. Brown, in listing the problems surrounding the seven churches, enumerates three in particular: false teaching, persecution, and complacency. Besides false teaching in Pergamum, a persecution for the death of a witness to Jesus named Antipas is mentioned. A key toward understanding the message to this church is the expression "Satan's throne." This refers to the imperial cult which had been established here, though there are also possibilities that it refers to an ancient altar erected to Zeus, or the temple of the goddess Roma, the imperial bench or tribunal, the temple of Asklepios, or simply as the center of religion wherein idolatry and sexual immorality are fostered.

Another fact about Pergamum is that it had one of the finest libraries in the world at that time, rivaling Alexandria in Egypt. The modern term "parchment" comes from the city of Pergamum. This was used for sheepskins on which were written sacred or juridical texts. The city had originally been dedicated to Athena the victory bearer. Thanks to the final editing of Revelation it is today perhaps "the most famous place of Asia" (see Aune, pp. 180-181; 194-195).

Through the angel or messenger sent to the church of Pergamum, Christ speaks with words that are as sharp as two-edged swords. Symbolically this refers to the divine truth of which Jesus is witness and revealer (see Heb 4:12). His divine truth cuts through all satanic deceit, human fabrication, or lies. Brown's insight that the problem in Pergamum is false teaching makes sense since everything connected with the throne or person of Satan is filled with lies, deceit, and trickery. The people of Pergamum have been faithful and truthful witnesses. Antipas, a citizen of Pergamum, was martyred for his fidelity to the truths of Christianity. Jesus Christ is also portrayed here as the "faithful witness" who appeared in the inaugural vision (Rv 1:5a).

There are similarities to the problem of false teaching and idolatry and immorality in this community. These difficulties are suggested by the symbolic name of Balaam who is involved in the book of Numbers (22-24) with idolatry and sexual immorality. He tried to seduce Israel through Balak, a prophet. The Nicolaitans are also mentioned. They, too, as we saw above are involved with heretical practices of a cultic and sexual nature. Such things seem to haunt every civilization under newer forms. In these matters the words of wisdom from Ecclesiastes are recalled, "There is nothing new under the sun." Revelation 2:14 is explicit: "some there hold to the teaching of Balaam, who taught Balak to put a stumbling block (skandalon) before the people of Israel, so that they would eat food sacrificed to idols and practice fornication." Moreover, a teaching (didache) similar to that of the Nicolaitans is expressly stated.

The call to conversion is given to the community (*metanoie-son*). Otherwise, they are threatened to be decimated by the sword of truth coming from the mouth of Jesus, the true witness and revealer of God. A twofold symbol of promise is given to those who are victorious over these false teachings — manna and a white stone with a personal name known only to the victorious recipient. Eternal life, rewarded to such a believer, is symbolized by the manna and the white stone. Once again, the community is urged to listen to the prompting of the Spirit speaking to all of the churches (Rv 2:17).

The Church at Thyatira (Rv 2:18-29)

Thyatira is another ancient city whose name now is Akhisar. It is some 60 to 70 miles northwest of Smyrna. During the first century this city was involved in many mercantile businesses: dye-makers (Lydia, Paul's first convert from Asia may have learned her art of dye-making at Thyatira [Ac 16:14-15,40]), shoemakers, bakers, tanners, coppersmiths, wool merchants, clothiers, etc. Later in Revelation we see how rich in trade such a city may have been by the wonder and the woes of the sailors and merchants who write in anguish over the fall of Rome and its satellites (see chapters 17 and 18). The composition of chapter 18 is a dynamic dirge — showing the greatness of Babylon (Rome) and lamenting its ultimate fall to ruin.

Brown sees the key problem at Thyatira consisting in false teaching which results in sexual promiscuity and idolatry. A clue to false teachings is the biblical name Jezebel, a Canaanite Queen and wife of King Ahab of Israel (1 K 18-19; 2 K 9). She was the enemy of the prophet Elijah. In Revelation Jezebel seems to be a symbol for the Nicolaitan sect who induces Christians to partake of food offered to idols or the emperor and to indulge in sexual promiscuity.

Thyatira had no temple. It was used as a garrison city by the Romans. Perhaps, because of the influx of Roman soldiers, Thyatira became a boom town for merchants. The fact that it had many guilds shows that it was a thriving city with great diversity in its populace as compared to the other six cities.

The only time that the title Son of God is used in Revelation for the person of Christ is to be found here in the address to the angel of the church in Thyatira. It definitely reflects what was mentioned already in the first chapter (Rv 1:13-15) which is an allusion to the son of man vision in Daniel 7:9 and 7:13. Thus these titles used for Christ are similar to the ones that were described in the initial visionary experience of John of Patmos.

The community of Christians is praised for four works: love (*agape*), faith (*pistis*), service (*diakônia*), and patient endurance (*hypomone*). This indicates that the Christians were as active in their ministries as the guilds were in their merchandising. These four gifts or works are signs of a successful and integrated church; this holds true for churches today.

The admonition in this letter against "Jezebel" is strong and judgmental. She and her followers will experience death. Christ as judge or all powerful *Pantocrator* is the searcher of minds and hearts. The scene recalls Paul's difficulty with the permissiveness of the Christians at Corinth in the case of incest (1 Cor 5). Like a lump of yeast the whole community could be rendered impure should Jezebel continue to be tolerated.

A promise is made which recalls the messianic message of Psalm 2:8-9. The Christians will be given spiritual power over the nations and will also possess the light of the morning star, another symbol for Christ as the light for all nations.

Food for the Journey:

Hebrews 10:32-39

[32]But recall those earlier days when, after you had been enlightened, you endured a hard struggle with sufferings, [33]sometimes being publicly exposed to abuse and persecution, and sometimes being partners with those so treated. [34]For you felt compassion for

those who were in prison, and you cheerfully accepted the plundering of your possessions, knowing that you yourselves possessed something better and more lasting. [35]Do not, therefore, abandon that confidence of yours; it brings a great reward. [36]For you need endurance, so that when you have done the will of God, you may receive what was promised. [37]For yet "in a very little while, the one who is coming will come and will not delay; [38]but my righteous one will live by faith. My soul takes no pleasure in anyone who shrinks back." [39]But we are not among those who shrink back and so are lost, but among those who have faith and so are saved.

Revelation 3:1-21

[1]"And to the angel of the church in Sardis write: 'These are the words of him who has the seven spirits of God and the seven stars: "I know your works; you have the reputation of being alive, but you are dead. [2]Wake up, and strengthen what remains and is on the point of death, for I have not found your works perfect in the sight of my God. [3]Remember then what you received and heard; obey it, and repent. If you do not wake up, I will come like a thief, and you will not know at what hour I will come to you. [4]Yet you have still a few persons in Sardis who have not soiled their clothes; they will walk with me, dressed in white, for they are worthy. [5]If you conquer, you will be clothed like them in white robes, and I will not blot your name out of the Book of Life; I will confess your name before my Father and before his angels. [6]Let anyone who has an ear listen to what the Spirit is saying to the churches."
[7]"And to the angel of the church in Philadelphia write:

'These are the words of the holy one, the true one,
who has the key of David,
who opens and no one will shut,
who shuts and no one opens:

[8]"I know your works. Look, I have set before you an open door, which no one is able to shut. I know that you have but little power, and yet you have kept my word and have not denied my name. [9]I will make those of the synagogue of Satan who say that they are

Jews and are not, but are lying — I will make them come and bow down before your feet, and they will learn that I have loved you. [10]Because you have kept my word of patient endurance, I will keep you from the hour of trial that is coming on the whole world to test the inhabitants of the earth. [11]I am coming soon; hold fast to what you have, so that no one may seize your crown. [12]If you conquer, I will make you a pillar in the temple of my God; you will never go out of it. I will write on you the name of my God, and the name of the city of my God, the new Jerusalem that comes down from my God out of heaven, and my own new name. [13]Let anyone who has an ear listen to what the Spirit is saying to the churches."

[14]"And to the angel of the church in Laodicea write: 'The words of the Amen, the faithful and true witness, the origin of God's creation:

[15]"I know your works; you are neither cold nor hot. I wish that you were either cold or hot. [16]But, because you are lukewarm, and neither cold nor hot, I am about to spit you out of my mouth. [17]For you say, 'I am rich, I have prospered, and I need nothing.' You do not realize that you are wretched, pitiable, poor, blind, and naked. [18]Therefore I counsel you to buy from me gold refined by fire so that you may be rich; and white robes to clothe you and to keep the shame of your nakedness from being seen; and salve to anoint your eyes so that you may see. [19]I reprove and discipline those whom I love. Be earnest, therefore, and repent. [20]Listen! I am standing at the door, knocking; if you hear my voice and open the door, I will come in to you and eat with you, and you with me. [21]To the one who conquers I will give a place with me on my throne, just as I myself conquered and sat down with my Father on his throne.'"

The Church at Sardis (Rv 3:1-6)

Sardis is one of the most celebrated cities in ancient Anatolia (Turkey). It is 45 miles east of Smyrna. During the time period of Revelation it was the capital of Lydia. It is famous for its wealth in gold and its woven textiles. Several noteworthy architectural structures in Sardis are the temple of Artemia (Diana, goddess of the hunt) and the largest Jewish synagogue called Beth Alpha. Sardis' citadel is the 1500 foot Mount Tmolus. Despite its boast as being impregnable, it was taken twice by surprise, once in 546 B.C.E. by Cyrus and again by Antiochus in 195 B.C.E. Hence, the admonition "Watch!" in this letter would be well understood by the inhabitants of Sardis.

The one who speaks prophetically to this church is described as having the seven spirits of God and the seven stars. It is Jesus as *Pantocrator* over the universal Church and, more specifically, over the church of Sardis which is the focus of this passage. This title, like the others, has already been mentioned in Rv 1:20. Here Jesus the Revealer is meant.

Brown mentions that complacency or apathy is the problem besetting Sardis. As a church it is not vigilant against the allurements of the empire. Nothing good is said about this church; hence the emphasis is on warning. The warning is severe and overwhelming: "Wake up! And strengthen what remains and is on the point of death, for I have not found your works perfect in the sight of my God" (Rv 3:2).

Several times during the visionary experience of the seer from Patmos, words similar to the sayings found in Matthew and Luke come to mind. Our author could be relying on an oral tradition or he may have borrowed the expressions from the eschatological vigilance called for by Jesus in the Gospels. Here, the Lord describes himself as a thief coming at night (see Mt 24:42-44; Lk 12:39-40). The one who confesses Jesus "before" or "in the face of" all will be commended (cf. Mt 10:32 and Lk 12:8). The same preposition (*enôpian*) for "before" or "in the face of" is unique to Revelation. This may favor an oral tradition over a direct dependence on a written Gospel. Four commands are given: Awake! Strengthen! Remember! Repent! A lethargy resembling death seems to have settled over this community. The clarion voice of Jesus is calling them back to life just as He had summoned Lazarus from the tomb.

The only encouraging message is that there are a few in Sardis who have maintained their innocence; they are dressed in the white clothing of the righteous and the victorious.

The book of life is taken from the Hebrew Bible and refers to the listing of those who are righteous before God. It is a metaphor for eternal life and salvation. Later in Revelation, the visionary explains this expression: "Also another book was opened, the Book of Life. And the dead were judged according to their works, as recorded in the books" (Rv 20:12).

The Church at Philadelphia (Rv 3:7-13)

This Asian city of *Philadelphia* is located 28 miles southeast of Sardis and 60 miles east of Smyrna at the foot of Mount Tmolus. It was founded by Altalus II Philadelphus of Pergamum with the purpose of being an "open door" (Rv 3:8) for Greek culture in these more remote places of Asia. Like twelve other cities it was destroyed by an earthquake in 17 C.E. and rebuilt by Tiberius and renamed Neo-Caesarea. Later under Vespasian it was again rebuilt with Flavia attached to its name.

The region was known for its vineyards because of the volcanic quality of the soil. Philadelphia was also on the route coming from Rome thus continuing to be an "open door" for cultural exchange. The church at Philadelphia is poor and weak, but faithful to its call like the former remnant of Israel which was totally dependent upon God.

Christ — who, in addressing this church in the sixth letter of Revelation is called the "holy one, the true one, who has the key of David, who opens and no one will shut, who shuts and no one opens" — has already been announced in chapter one verse five as the true witness and in verse eighteen as having the keys over death and Hades. The citation of having the keys of David to open and close the door is from Isaiah 22:22 and is a symbol for messianic power to receive the righteous into God's Kingdom and to keep out those who are not among the faithful. The metaphor continues in verse eight where Christ, the Messiah, confirms this open door of hope for the future (cf. Jr 20:11).

The problem facing this particular church is opposition and some form of persecution which the false Jews from the Synagogue of Satan, the adversary, inflicts on these Jewish Christians. Shortly after the book of Revelation was written Ignatius of Antioch stayed in Philadelphia on his way to Rome and suggests there was a Judaizing force in this city.

There is nothing bad said about this Christian community. They are encouraged to persevere in their fidelity. A beautiful expression is given to them which suggests that even conversions to Christianity will come about because they — possibly the Jews — will learn that Christ has loved them (*hoti ego agapesa se*). The Parousia, or Coming of the Lord, is predicted and words recalling the last eschatological theme of the Lord's Prayer seems to be behind verses ten and eleven.... "I will keep you from the hour of trial that is coming on the whole world to test the inhabitants of the earth."

The metaphor of the New Jerusalem descending from above will be fully elaborated upon in chapters 21 and 22.

The Church in Laodicea (Rv 3:14-22)

Laodicea is situated in the fertile valley of the Lycus River on an important trade route. It is 100 miles east of Ephesus and just 11 miles from Colossae in Phrygia. Again it is one of the cities disturbed by earthquakes, but it managed to survive and became prosperous during the time of the writing of the book of Revelation. It was famous for its clothing made of black wool. Laodicea is mentioned five times in the Epistle to the Colossians (2:1; 4:13,15,16 [2x]).

Close to Laodicia are Hierapolis and Colossae. Waters which were medicinal "hot springs" were found at Hieropolis, while "cold water" from Colossae was noted for its purity. Laodicea suffered the common plight of hard tepid water. This could have led to the use of appropriate metaphoric language in this letter referring to the lukewarm condition of the Christian community at Laodicea.

The words used to describe Christ in the address are the Amen, faithful and true witness, and the ruler or beginning of God's creation, and are partially found in the introduction of chapter one verse five. Though the word Amen is found in Rv 1:6 it is not applied directly to Christ as here. The final phrase about Christ as the beginning has some similarities at the end of verse five, but Aune states these attributes are not drawn from the Patmos vision in 1:9-20 (Aune, 52A, p. 263).

Nothing good is said about this community which is mired in its tepidity. In fact, the status of the church is despicable as understood by the saying "you are neither cold nor hot, but lukewarm; I am about to spit you out of my mouth... you are wretched, pitiable, poor, blind, and naked" (Rv 3:17cd).

An expanded exhortation is given to this complacent, lukewarm and lethargic community. The admonition could possibly lead to a cure of the ills mentioned above. These conditions would have prevented people from entering the temple in Jerusalem and may have been an allusion to such a prohibition on the part of the Revealer. They would not be able as naked, blind, and poor to enter the New Jerusalem. This language is not meant to be offensive, but was typical of the strong biblical language used in the centuries before the common era and also during the period of the formation of the New Testament. The meaning of the symbols would be understood by the people of John's time.

Rv 3:20 presents a problem for the exegete since the metaphor seems to be so unique. There are similarities to two parables found in Lk 12:35-38 and Mk 13:33-37. Christ is speaking personally here in this powerful metaphor; for that reason Joachim Jeremias calls it a deparabolized expression. However, it is characteristic of this book of the New Testament to be quite fluid and plastic in its symbolic language and imagery.

I am reminded of the scene of Jesus washing the feet of his disciples before sitting down with them to a meal (Jn 13:1-17). Here the imagery is of one knocking at the door waiting for a response and an opening to the home. The patience and outreach of the Lord is breathtaking. The meal symbolism is perfect for the messianic banquet prefigured in the Church by the Eucharist. Is this what is implied in the imagery? I would hope so.

In a marvelous book entitled *Tales of the End* by David Barr, the following description of the "Laodicean letter" is accurate and helpful for the reader:

"The Laodicean letter emphasizes true and false perception, with the one who is the faithful and true witness giving an analysis of their situation that is wholly at odds with their own analysis. They think themselves to be rich and without need; the witness says they are poor, blind, naked, and wretched. They are advised to buy gold, white clothes, and eye salve. The letter closes with a poignant scene of the human one standing outside a closed door and promising anyone who would open the door that they will dine together. The victor is promised a heavenly enthronement just as Jesus was victorious and received such a heavenly throne." (Barr, D., *Tales of the End*, p. 45).

Finally, in summarizing the situation of the churches addressed, R.E. Brown says succinctly: "The overarching message that spans the seven letters and matches the theme of the rest of the book is to stand firm and make no concession to what the author designates as evil. The optimistic promises to the victor in each letter fit the goal of encouragement that is characteristic of apocalyptic" (Brown, p. 786).

Listening to the Spirit to what is being said to the churches results in sharing in the victory of Jesus the Christ over evil, Satan, and death. We can hear Jesus in the final promise saying: "To the one who conquers I will give a place with me on my throne, just as I myself conquered and sat down with my Father on his throne" (Rv 3:21).

Food for the Journey:

1 Peter 2:4-10

> [4]Come to him, a living stone, though rejected by mortals yet chosen and precious in God's sight, and [5]like living stones, let yourselves be built into a spiritual house, to be a holy priesthood, to offer spiritual sacrifices acceptable to God through Jesus Christ. [6]For it stands in scripture: "See, I am laying in Zion a stone, a cornerstone chosen and precious; and whoever believes in him will not be put to shame." [7]To you then who believe, he is precious; but for those who do not believe, "The stone that the builders rejected has become the very head of the corner," [8]and "A stone that makes them stumble, and a rock that makes them fall." They stumble because they disobey the word, as they were destined to do. [9]But you are a chosen race, a royal priesthood, a holy nation, God's own people, in order that you may proclaim the mighty acts of him who called you out of darkness into his marvelous light. [10]Once you were not a people, but now you are God's people; once you had not received mercy, but now you have received mercy.

CHAPTER THREE

THE OPENING OF THE SCROLL OF WORSHIP
(Rv 4-7)

Revelation 4:1-11

¹After this I looked, and there in heaven a door stood open! And the first voice, which I had heard speaking to me like a trumpet, said, "Come up here, and I will show you what must take place after this." ²At once I was in the spirit, and there in heaven stood a throne, with one seated on the throne! ³And the one seated there looks like jasper and carnelian, and around the throne is a rainbow that looks like an emerald. ⁴Around the throne are twenty-four thrones, and seated on the thrones are twenty-four elders, dressed in white robes, with golden crowns on their heads. ⁵Coming from the throne are flashes of lightning, and rumblings and peals of thunder, and in front of the throne burn seven flaming torches, which are the seven spirits of God; ⁶and in front of the throne there is something like a sea of glass, like crystal.

Around the throne, and on each side of the throne, are four living creatures, full of eyes in front and behind: ⁷the first living creature like a lion, the second living creature like an ox, the third living creature with a face like a human face, and the fourth living creature like a flying eagle. ⁸And the four living creatures, each of them with six wings, are full of eyes all around and inside. Day and night without ceasing they sing, "Holy, holy, holy, the Lord God the Almighty, who was and is and is to come." ⁹And whenever the living creatures give glory and honor and thanks to the one who is seated on the throne, who lives forever and ever, [10]the twenty-four elders fall before the one who is seated on the throne and worship the one who lives forever and ever; they cast their crowns before the throne, singing, [11]"You are worthy, our Lord and God, to receive glory and honor and power, for you created all things, and by your will they existed and were created."

John of Patmos speaks:

You are aware how much I longed to celebrate the Passover supper of the Lamb with the congregations of the seven churches. All of a sudden I think the Lord gave me this privilege in another surprising way. I was wafted to heaven where I saw an open door. As Paul said in one of his letters to the Corinthians, I was not sure I was in the body or out of the body. I fell into a trance that enabled me to experience the heavenly throne room. God's magnificent presence and glory caught me in my ecstasy. Upon a white throne surrounded with precious stones, God was seated. An emerald-like rainbow wrapped around Him while twenty-four elders in white robes and gold wreaths worshiped. The seven blazing torches reminded me of the churches I had to address; the theophany continued with thunder, lightning and rumbling. I then saw four creatures which merged into what I had read from Ezekiel and Isaiah's ecstatic visions: a lion, an ox, a human figure and a flying eagle — ministers or masters of ceremonies before God. Each had six wings. They praised God and sang out three times, holy, holy, holy (*kadosha! kadosha! kadosha!*). Glory and honor and thanks belong to the one seated upon the throne. Even the twenty-four elders fell prostrate and cast their wreaths before the throne and joined the singing of the others in heaven. All worshiped God the creator of the heavens and the earth. Yes, this was a great way of celebrating the Lord's supper on a Sunday!

And then a large beautiful scroll appeared. Were the prophets to be read? But the scroll was sealed seven times from top to bottom and no one made a move to unseal it. I started to weep bitterly. Suddenly one of the elders tapped my shoulder and said, "The Lamb who is the Lion of Judah and the root of David will open the scroll for you." In the midst of the throne surrounded by the four living creatures and the elders I saw a stately and comely lamb that bore the marks of a lamb that had been slaughtered. It had seven horns and seven eyes (the seven spirits of God). This Lamb took the scroll and would eventually open the seals one by one.

I remembered that the Lord Jesus was the Paschal Lamb, the one who gave his life as a ransom for all of us. This was the heavenly re-enactment of the Lord's supper and somehow I was united with the seven churches through this glorious celebration. All in the heavens — countless angels and those surrounding the throne praised the Lamb proclaiming seven of his attributes: power, wealth, wisdom, might, honor, glory, and blessing! All of this praise resounded in a harmonious chorus that went on forever and ever. The four living creatures chanted Amen! and the elders fell down in worship.

One of the four living creatures motioned to me saying, "Come!" I then saw each of four seals opened by the Lamb. Four horses were revealed representing the calamities to be wrought upon earth. The rider on the white horse conquered people; the red horse with its rider brought war upon the earth; the black horse represented devastation of crops and nourishment; the last horse was pale green like a corpse. Death and Hades followed behind it.

What could such destructive forces signify? The fifth seal gave me the answer. As it was opened I saw the souls of those who were slaughtered because of the Word of God and their testimony to the Lamb. They were yearning for their fellow brothers and sisters on earth awaiting their own martyrdom. They cried out, "How long, Lord, holy and true one, must it be before you judge and avenge our blood?"

I watched as the sixth seal was opened. I remembered what Mark had recorded about Jesus and the happenings of the last day. An earthquake, an eclipse, and the moon turning blood red ripped open the skies like a scroll being flapped back. All on the earth cried for an end to their misery and they hid themselves in caves. How I hated my own cave!

Four angels at the four corners of the earth held back the winds from further devastation of the earth. Another angel had a seal from the living God which was to be used on the foreheads of God's faithful servants. Then a marvelous throng came before my eyes and I recognized twelve tribes of my own ancestral heritage. Only Dan was missing with the enumerated 144,000, but Manasseh took his place. Dan was missing because of his idolatry and similarity to the evil power over the churches.

More throngs of people came before me — the heavens were filled with them and they sang out in unison "Amen! Praise, glory and wisdom, thanksgiving and honor be to our God — forever and ever! Amen!"

One of the elders spoke to me and asked, "Who are these people in white?" I thought it to be an irritating question so I gave him my sharp reply, "You tell me; you certainly know who they are." He told me they were those who had been washed in the blood of the Lamb and now no longer would suffer any form of thirst, hunger, or pain. The Lamb led them as sheep to the waters of everlasting life in the heavens.

COMMENTARY

The Heavenly Worship (Rv 4:1-11)

The seer, after having sent the scroll of letters to the seven churches, returns to his initial experience. Line one contains an inclusion with the words "After this." The expression in Greek attests to a continuation of what was first experienced on the island of Patmos. It is the same angelic voice with the clarion sound of a trumpet inviting him to look into the heavens. Once peering into the open door he will be able to view what is to happen "after this" (verse 1). Then in spirit he sees someone sitting upon a throne in the heavens (verse 2). The vision is imbued with splendid colors resembling the brilliance of gems: jasper, sard stone, and emerald. Jasper is a deep dark green marble; sard is a reddish brown chalcedony; emerald is a bright rich green precious stone. The rainbow surrounding the One on the throne is not many colored but solely described as having a bright green hue. The visionary tells us what it was like to see these colors. As we move through Revelation we will experience a love for the description of nature and animate and inanimate forms of life. The visions are almost kaleidoscopic, always giving a new angle of descriptive color and meaning, yet, revolving around the same theme: Worship God... and God alone.

Verse 4 continues the description by mentioning that upon 24 thrones are seated 24 elders wearing golden crowns. Aune mentions in an excursus that there is no universal consensus about the identification of the 24 elders. The visionary does not identify them. Perhaps, the best solution is to see them representing the 24 priestly courses of the second temple described in 1 Ch 23:6; 24:7-18. The word elder (*presbyter* in Greek) came to be used for priest in the early Church. We are in the temple of the heavenly court which had its corresponding earthly image in the temple of Jerusalem. There are also 24 musicians in the temple. A third possibility is that they represent the twelve sons of Israel and their counterpart in Christianity, the twelve apostles. Their white robes symbolize holiness and victory. Their crowns are a confirmation of such an honor.

The glory of God (the one seated upon the throne) is emphasized by the theophany of lightning amidst seven lamps and seven heavenly spirits. All this is accompanied by thunder and voices. Undoubtedly, the experience of Moses on Mount Sinai comes to mind. (Ex 19:16). There are four such theophanies in Revelation besides: Rv 4:5a; 8:5c; 11:19c and 16:18-21. In addition to lightning, thunder, and voices, hail and earthquakes are part of some of the theophanies. The glory of God (*kabôd Yahweh*) is what John is experiencing. The visionary tells us the seven burning lamps are the seven spirits in front of the throne of God. These seven spirits are most likely the seven angels representing the seven guardians of the churches (Rv 1:4) or the seven torches of the Menorah. Aune sees an allusion to Zechariah 4:2: "He said to me, 'What do you see?' And I said, 'I see a lampstand all of gold, with a bowl on top of it; there are seven lamps on it, with seven lips on each of the lamps that are on top of it.'" In Zechariah it is an angel who is speaking; moreover, this prophet has stimulated the seer's mind throughout the book of Revelation.

Almost like a camera zooming in on the throne, always getting closer, now the seer describes four living creatures who will be mentioned 14 times in Revelation. These living beings are a combination of the ones described already in the vision of Ezekiel 1:5-25 and Isaiah 6:2, though later tradition would identify them with the four evangelists (Mark, the lion; Matthew, the man; Luke, the ox; John, the eagle). Here they are cherubim and serve God throughout Revelation as ministers of worship acting like deacons to make sure all is proper to the worship of God. The mention of their having eyes in front and behind emphasizes their awareness and fullness of knowledge. Four symbolizes the four corners of the then known earth or even the universe. Once again completeness and universality is what is called for in worshiping God from every location.

For a remarkable excursus on the four living creatures, the cherubim, see Aune's commentary on 4:7-8 (Aune, *Rev. Vol. 52A*, pp. 297-305). The four cherubim speak incessantly in praise of the one seated upon the throne using the same words as the seraphs in Isaiah 6:3. Holy! Holy! Holy! is the Lord God the Almighty (*Pantocrator* in place of hosts or armies). *Pantocrator* is used 5 times in Revelation. It is translated "the Almighty."

The phrase "who was and is and is to come" is a threefold description of the divinity used in Revelation for God, most often, and a few times for Jesus.

Verses 9-11 are the climax of this chapter. They present in heaven what should be happening in the seven churches when the community is gathered for worship. The four living creatures render perfect glory, and honor, and thanksgiving incessantly while the 24 elders cast off their crowns and fall down in prostration before the throne of God in the same spirit and cry out in praise: "Worthy are you, O Lord our God, to receive glory and honor and power because you have brought into being all things and by your will they existed and were created."

In summary, the fourth chapter is centered on the worship of God which takes place in the heavens. The marvelous and colorful description, together with the chant of the four living creatures and the praise of the 24 elders demonstrates that all living creatures of both former times (the Hebrew Scriptures) and of the present, the second testament (Christian Scriptures) are to worship the One who existed before and now is and will ever be forever. Amen.

Food for the Journey:

Isaiah 6:1-5

> [1]In the year that King Uzziah died, I saw the Lord sitting on a throne, high and lofty; and the hem of his robe filled the temple. [2]Seraphs were in attendance above him; each had six wings: with two they covered their faces, and with two they covered their feet, and with two they flew. [3]And one called to another and said: "Holy, holy, holy is the Lord of hosts; the whole earth is full of his glory." [4]The pivots on the thresholds shook at the voices of those who called, and the house filled with smoke. [5]And I said: "Woe is me! I am lost, for I am a man of unclean lips, and I live among a people of unclean lips; yet my eyes have seen the King, the Lord of hosts!"

Revelation 5:1-14

> [1]Then I saw in the right hand of the one seated on the throne a scroll written on the inside and on the back, sealed with seven seals; [2]and I saw a mighty angel proclaiming with a loud voice,

"Who is worthy to open the scroll and break its seals?" ³And no one in heaven or on earth or under the earth was able to open the scroll or to look into it. ⁴And I began to weep bitterly because no one was found worthy to open the scroll or to look into it. ⁵Then one of the elders said to me, "Do not weep. See, the Lion of the tribe of Judah, the Root of David, has conquered, so that he can open the scroll and its seven seals."

⁶Then I saw between the throne and the four living creatures and among the elders a Lamb standing as if it had been slaughtered, having seven horns and seven eyes, which are the seven spirits of God sent out into all the earth. ⁷He went and took the scroll from the right hand of the one who was seated on the throne. ⁸When he had taken the scroll, the four living creatures and the twenty-four elders fell before the Lamb, each holding a harp and golden bowls full of incense, which are the prayers of the saints. ⁹They sing a new song:

> "You are worthy to take the scroll
> and to open its seals,

¹⁰you have made them to be a kingdom and priests serving our God, and they will reign on earth."

¹¹Then I looked, and I heard the voice of many angels surrounding the throne and the living creatures and the elders; they numbered myriads of myriads and thousands of thousands, ¹²singing with full voice,

> "Worthy is the Lamb that was slaughtered
> to receive power and wealth and wisdom and might
> and honor and glory and blessing!"

¹³Then I heard every creature in heaven and on earth and under the earth and in the sea, and all that is in them, singing,

> "To the one seated on the throne and to the Lamb
> be blessing and honor and glory and might
> forever and ever!"

¹⁴And the four living creatures said, "Amen!" And the elders fell down and worshiped.

COMMENTARY

The Heavenly Temple and the Scroll and the Lamb
(Rv 5:1-14)

The heavenly vision continues but a new image is brought into focus. This is Jesus symbolized by the Paschal Lamb which has been slaughtered. It is the lamb who will open the scroll that has been secured by seven seals which no one in heaven or on earth or under the earth could open. This dramatic scene is part of the worship rendered to God and to the Lamb in heaven. It is a continuation of what is unfolding for the seer.

The scroll is central to what will be revealed in chapters six, seven, and eight, verse six. This chapter is the key to the unfolding of the plan of God in world history. Each seal which the Lamb breaks reveals in graphic detail the eschatological (the last or final) events as seen by the prophet experiencing the vision. No one on earth or heaven could break the seals. This declaration shows the reader that the Lamb who is sacrificed is a symbol of Jesus, who through his suffering, death, and resurrection, has accomplished what God wills for all of creation. Behind the seer's vision is the passover Lamb of Exodus 12 and the Suffering Servant of Isaiah 53. C. Stuhlmueller gives us a theme that is helpful in understanding the suffering servant and the Israel who follows him or is represented by him. Jesus is the agent of creative redemption; his followers are to assume the same role as had been given in the scroll to the churches.

Since Revelation is in its final redaction a Christian message, the Lamb is easily identified with Jesus, the Lamb of God who takes away the sin of the world (cf. Jn 1:29). Jesus also fulfills the Messianic titles by being identified with the tribe of Judah under the symbol of a lion; we see a paradoxical combination of lion and lamb, but symbolism is fluid and plastic and combines opposites in a revelatory way. Jesus also is of the root of the stem of David; these Messianic titles are taken from Genesis 49:9-10 and from Isaiah 11:1,10. Jesus, however, is a suffering Messiah despite the kingly origins of his lineage (see Mt 1:1-17; Rm 1:1-3). Jesus, as one of the 24 elders will tell us, is the one who is worthy to unseal the scroll, breaking each seal one by one, enabling the visionary to see what is to happen as salvation history unfolds. There is a smooth mixing of eschatology, soteriology, and christology in this chapter. We have already been prepared for this trial by chapter one and the titles or description given to Jesus.

The word "victory" is at the core of Jesus' power. He alone conquers all forms of evil: sin, death, and all demonic forces. Revelation has the word "victory" 17 times out of 28 references in the New Testament. It always is used with reference to Jesus or those who are following him through courageous witness and enduring perseverance.

The Lamb has seven horns and seven eyes which are the seven spirits sent out all over the world. I take this to mean the universal plan of God for the entire Church represented by the seven who have been given a scroll of letters. Ultimately, it is a call to all believers to participate in the victory of the Lamb.

Upon taking the scroll from the one sitting on the throne, the four living creatures and the 24 elders who have harps and vials of incense, join in singing a new song of victory to the Lamb. We are told the vials of incense are the prayers of the saints. Once again, the "communion of saints" both in heaven and on earth join in worshiping God and the Lamb. We are again at the dominant theme of Revelation: "Worship God." The song brings out the call for every tribe, tongue, people, and nation who are priests and kings through the victory of the Lamb, to worship God and the Lamb.

The voices of all in heaven resound with a powerful response in verse 12: "Worthy is the Lamb that was slaughtered to receive power and wealth and wisdom and might and honor and glory and blessing."

The chant of the heavenly choir resounds to every part of God's creation and, in a mystical moment, all creatures are united in praising God now for the third time (verse 13): "To the one seated on the throne, and to the lamb, be blessing and honor and glory and might forever and ever!"

The worship before the throne is brought to a close with the liturgical Amen! while the four living creatures and the elders fall in adoration before the throne. These scenes of worship enable the seer and the readers (listeners) to have a sense of hope despite what will now take place as the Lamb begins to open the seven seals.

Food for the Journey:

Psalm 148:1-6,13

[1]Praise the Lord! Praise the Lord from the heavens; praise him in the heights! [2]Praise him, all his angels; praise him, all his host! [3]Praise him, sun and moon; praise him, all you shining stars! [4]Praise him, you highest heavens, and you waters above the heavens! [5]Let them praise the name of the Lord, for he commanded and they were created. [6]He established them forever and ever; he fixed their bounds, which cannot be passed. [13]Let them praise the name of the Lord, for his name alone is exalted; his glory is above earth and heaven.

Revelation 6:1-17

[1]Then I saw the Lamb open one of the seven seals, and I heard one of the four living creatures call out, as with a voice of thunder, "Come!" [2]I looked, and there was a white horse! Its rider had a bow; a crown was given to him, and he came out conquering and to conquer.

[3]When he opened the second seal, I heard the second living creature call out, "Come!" [4]And out came another horse, bright red; its rider was permitted to take peace from the earth, so that people would slaughter one another; and he was given a great sword.

[5]When he opened the third seal, I heard the third living creature call out, "Come!" I looked, and there was a black horse! Its rider held a pair of scales in his hand, [6]and I heard what seemed to be a voice in the midst of the four living creatures saying, "A

quart of wheat for a day's pay, and three quarts of barley for a day's pay, but do not damage the olive oil and the wine!"

[7]When he opened the fourth seal, I heard the voice of the fourth living creature call out, "Come!" [8]I looked and there was a pale green horse! Its rider's name was Death, and Hades followed with him; they were given authority over a fourth of the earth, to kill with sword, famine, and pestilence, and by the wild animals of the earth.

[9]When he opened the fifth seal, I saw under the altar the souls of those who had been slaughtered for the word of God and for the testimony they had given; [10]they cried out with a loud voice, "Sovereign Lord, holy and true, how long will it be before you judge and avenge our blood on the inhabitants of the earth?" [11]They were each given a white robe and told to rest a little longer, until the number would be complete both of their fellow servants and of their brothers and sisters, who were soon to be killed as they themselves had been killed.

[12]When he opened the sixth seal, I looked, and there came a great earthquake; the sun became black as sackcloth, the full moon became like blood, [13]and the stars of the sky fell to the earth as the fig tree drops its winter fruit when shaken by a gale. [14]The sky vanished like a scroll rolling itself up, and every mountain and island was removed from its place. [15]Then the kings of the earth and the magnates and the generals and the rich and the powerful, and everyone, slave and free, hid in the caves and among the rocks of the mountains, [16]calling to the mountains and rocks, "Fall on us and hide us from the face of the one seated on the throne and from the wrath of the Lamb; [17]for the great day of their wrath has come, and who is able to stand?"

COMMENTARY

The Seals (Rv 6)

The seven seals are preludes to the eschatological drama that is about to unfold. In this chapter, six of the seven seals are opened by the Lamb; each one of the seals unleashes various forms of havoc upon the people of the earth and upon various forms of life, animate and inanimate. These plagues remind us of the ones inflicted upon Egypt and Pharaoh in the Book of Exodus.

The scrolls are unraveled in chapters 6:1-8:1. The events and catastrophes are meant for the non-distant future. Though described in language from the past (the Hebrew Scriptures and the Apocalyptic and judgment scenes in the Synoptics [Mk 13:3-8, 24-27; Mt 24:8-14; Lk 21:12-19,25]) the future eschatological plan of God is what the seer divines from the loosed seals.

The first four seals (Rv 6:1-8)

Though not always logical, there are, nevertheless, certain orderly patterns written in symbolic language and taken from apocalyptic sources from the Hebrew Scriptures, the Christian Scriptures and inter-testamental apocalyptic works (Jewish apocalyptic). These sources are worked over creatively and with great skill by John of Patmos.

The famous four horsemen (cavaliers) appear for the first time in the prophet Zechariah (1:8-11; 6:1-8). There is also a divisional pattern of 4+3 seen in the revelation obtained from the seven seals, and also from the trumpet visions (8:2-9; 11:15-18). This inner consistency of Revelation is another key toward its interpretation. Detailed structured outlines like those provided by Aune in his monumental commentary demonstrate this consistency of the author of Revelation and provide a review of what each chapter entails. (See, for example, Chapter 6: Aune, Vol. 52B, pp. 386-389).

In another masterful work on Revelation (*Tales of the End: A Narrative Commentary on the Book of Revelation*), David L. Barr shows the reader five levels within the narrative at this juncture:

> We should remind ourselves of how deeply into the narrative we are. We have left the first level (John addressing the reader), gone through the second level (John of Patmos),

the third level (John's vision of heaven), to the fifth level (things seen by characters in the scene John sees in heaven). All the actions, stemming from the scroll occur at this narrative level (p. 81).

The first seal (Rv 6:1-2) is opened by the Lamb, while one of the living creatures (possibly the lion) roars "Come!" At once a rider on a white horse comes forth. The symbol of his having a bow in his hands suggests a Parthian warrior. During the historical time of the Apocalypse, the Parthians were the dreaded foe of the Romans. Christians and Jews probably hoped for some form of deliverance from the Romans through these fierce bowman who rode swiftly and targeted accurately. They are being victorious and would continue to conquer the oppressors. The white horse is also symbolic of victory and righteousness. The conquering victor would ride into the decimated areas upon a white horse. Most scholars warn us not to identify this rider with the Christ who also will appear on a white horse (Rv 19:11). The icon for Christ is not the bow but the two-edged sword of truth which issues from his mouth (Heb 4:12; Rv 1:16; 3:14). The color white is used 19 times in Revelation — usually as a sign of victory over oppression, death, or evil (Satan).

The second seal (Rv 6:3-4) follows exactly the pattern of the first. A second living creature (one of the *cherubim*) cries out, "Come!" and a ruddy colored horse is loosed. The rider is carrying a sword and takes peace away from the world while creating warfare among peoples. Red is the color of warfare in biblical symbolism; it also denotes the shedding of blood especially in warfare symbolized here by the large sword.

The third seal (6:5-6) has a living creature calling out, "Come!" and a black horse appears with a rider holding a scale in his hands. The context tells us why. There shall be a time of famine when a day's wages will be able to purchase only a small measure (a quart) of wheat, or three measures of the bread of the poor, barley. The staples of olive oil and wine are to be spared.

The final cavalier (Rv 6:7-8) breaks forth personified as Death and accompanied by Hades (the realm of the dead or Sheol). A fourth of the earth is to be devastated by this ugly colored horse and its rider. It is a pus color like a cadaver, or pale green. The earth is "killed" with pestilence and death itself; even the beasts are not spared.

At this point, I would like to summarize the key toward the time element in the Apocalypse, by citing another excellent commentator: Adela Yarbro Collins:

> Beginning with Chapter 6, it is very difficult to link the visions of the Apocalypse with specific events and to discern a detailed chronological outline. In some visions, the original Greek text shifts from future to past to present in an apparently random fashion. These characteristics show that the Apocalypse should not be read as an orderly prediction of a series of events. Rather, it is a poetic vision which uses future language to express something about the nature of reality, to interpret the present (*The Apocalypse, New Testament Message 22*, Glazier, Wilmington, Delaware, 1979, p. 43).

The fifth seal (6:9-11) is a vision of the souls under the heavenly altar who have suffered martyrdom because of their witness to the word of God and thereby gave up their lives for the truth of God's revelation. The word "witness" in Greek is *martyr*. In its noun and verbal forms it is used 19 times in Revelation. The early Christians saw martyrdom as the perfect form of witness to Christ. Ignatius of Antioch who lived during the early second century and knew of the seven churches is the perfect example of one who longed for martyrdom and who prayed that he be not taken from this crowning witness to Jesus, his Savior. This short pericope of the fifth seal gives us a glimpse into the victory of martyrs now near to God interceding for those on earth who are suffering extreme persecution.

Their white robes symbolize their worthiness, integrity, and victory over the evil oppressors who put them to death. Almost any saint from these martyrologies could be used as an example of how many early Christians gave their lives for Christ.

The Sixth Seal (Rv 6:12-17)

A powerful theophany takes place as the sixth seal is released. It is a cosmic scene: earthquakes, a solar eclipse, stars dropping from the sky like figs falling from the trees. Even the sky — pictured as a blue iron vault folds up like a scroll. In 17 C.E. an earthquake had shaken twelve cities in Asia Minor. Some of them were the cities named in chapters 1-3. Both in Jewish and Christian apocalyptic literature such cosmic descriptions are frequently given. There is a similar apocalypse in Mark's Gospel, 13:24-27. The great day of God's wrath was captured in the pre-Vatican II liturgical hymn, *Dies Irae*. This medieval hymn was based on Joel. Here in Revelation that prophet could also have been the source for the wrath of the Lamb. This day of judgment was aimed at the wicked (1 Cor 5:5; 1 Th 5:2; 2 Th 2:2; 2 P 3:10). Many hid or ran for the caves in the earth — even the just (cf. Heb 11:39).

Food for the Journey:

Zechariah 1:7-12

> [7]On the twenty-fourth day of the eleventh month, the month of Shebat, in the second year of Darius, the word of the Lord came to the prophet Zechariah son of Berechiah son of Iddo; and Zechariah said, [8]"In the night I saw a man riding on a red horse! He was standing among the myrtle trees in the glen; and behind him were red, sorrel, and white horses." [9]Then I said, "What are these, my lord?" The angel who talked with me said to me, "I will show you what they are." [10]So the man who was standing among the myrtle trees answered, "They are those whom the Lord has sent to patrol the earth." [11]Then they spoke to the angel of the Lord who was standing among the myrtle trees, "We have pa-

trolled the earth, and lo, the whole earth remains at peace." [12]Then the angel of the Lord said, "O Lord of hosts, how long will you withhold mercy from Jerusalem and the cities of Judah, with which you have been angry these seventy years?"

Revelation 7:1-17

[1]After this I saw four angels standing at the four corners of the earth, holding back the four winds of the earth so that no wind could blow on earth or sea or against any tree. [2]I saw another angel ascending from the rising of the sun, having the seal of the living God, and he called with a loud voice to the four angels who had been given power to damage earth and sea, [3]saying, "Do not damage the earth or the sea or the trees, until we have marked the servants of our God with a seal on their foreheads." [4]And I heard the number of those who were sealed, one hundred forty-four thousand, sealed out of every tribe of the people of Israel: [5]From the tribe of Judah twelve thousand sealed, from the tribe of Reuben twelve thousand, from the tribe of Gad twelve thousand, [6]from the tribe of Asher twelve thousand, from the tribe of Naphtali twelve thousand, from the tribe of Manasseh twelve thousand, [7]from the tribe of Simeon twelve thousand, from the tribe of Levi twelve thousand, from the tribe of Issachar twelve thousand, [8]from the tribe of Zebulun twelve thousand, from the tribe of Joseph twelve thousand, from the tribe of Benjamin twelve thousand sealed.

[9]After this I looked, and there was a great multitude that no one could count, from every nation, from all tribes and peoples and languages, standing before the throne and before the Lamb, robed in white, with palm branches in their hands. [10]They cried out in a loud voice, saying, "Salvation belongs to our God who is seated on the throne, and to the Lamb!" [11]And all the angels stood around the throne and around the elders and the four living creatures, and they fell on their faces before the throne and worshiped God, [12]singing, "Amen! Blessing and glory and wisdom and

thanksgiving and honor and power and might be to our God forever and ever! Amen."

[13]Then one of the elders addressed me, saying, "Who are
these, robed in white, and where have they come from?" [14]I said
to him, "Sir, you are the one that knows." Then he said to me,
"These are they who have come out of the great ordeal; they have
washed their robes and made them white in the blood of the Lamb.
[15]For this reason they are before the throne of God, and worship
him day and night within his temple, and the one who is seated
on the throne will shelter them. [16]They will hunger no more, and
thirst no more; the sun will not strike them, nor any scorching
heat; [17]for the Lamb at the center of the throne will be their shepherd, and he will guide them to springs of the water of life, and
God will wipe away every tear from their eyes."

COMMENTARY

The 144,000 of Israel sealed who worship God and the Lamb (Rv 7:1-17)

This chapter may be seen as consisting of two distinct scenes:
Rv 7:1-8 is the sealing of the twelve tribes of Israel, each of which
consists of 12,000; however, the tribe of Dan is not mentioned.
Perhaps, this scene attests to the election and choice of God for
Israel. The fidelity of Israel is represented by the twelve thousand
from each tribe.

The second scene consists of the universal call of all nations
to worship God. Nation, tribe, people, and language symbolize this
universal call. The New Israel is the Church.

Revelation 7:1-8

There is a slight variation suggested by the use of "after this."
The winds represent the four locations of the earth which are un-

der the control of four powerful angels. They restrain the winds from harming the earth, the sea, or the forest. Another angel arises from the east and calls out to the four that he must first mark with a signet the foreheads of those who are faithful to God from among the twelve tribes of Israel. This marking probably is similar to that suggested in Ezekiel wherein the faithful Israelites are signed with a *taw* (similar to a "T"). Scholars are convinced this is not the mark of baptism. The fact that emphasis is put on Israel's twelve tribes suggests rather the election and choice of Israel by God. Those who are faithful worshipers are given this special mark. It seems that this would take place on earth because of the impending and imminent trials and persecutions mentioned in the text; on the other hand there is a continuation of the vision taking place in heaven before the throne of God. Moreover, these faithful have been linked to what follows. It seems they, too, are among those "who have come out of the great ordeal; they have washed their robes and made them white in the blood of the Lamb" (7:14).

The best solution that scholars suggest about the scene of the 144,000 and also of the countless numbers from among the rest of the world's nations is that these scenes are "a proleptic vision of the future eschatological consummation" (Beckwith, Zahn, Mounce, Prigent and Giesen). This means in ordinary language that the representation of the future situation of the faithful 144,000 is anticipated by what the seer experiences in his vision even though the present reality may entail ordeals here on earth which the faithful ones are to experience.

The list of the twelve tribes in Revelation contains the mention of Levi which normally was omitted because of the dedication the Levites had to the Temple for worship; they did not possess land as did the other eleven tribes. Dan, however, is omitted. Speculation has it that because of the apostasy of the tribe of Dan, the tribe is omitted. St. Irenaeus of Lyon writing in the third century mentioned that the Anti-Christ would come from the tribe of Dan. Possibly this may spring from the fact that Dan is compared to a snake by the wayside, a viper on the path that bites the heels of the horse and its rider falls backward" (see Gn 49:17). There are several lists of the twelve tribes in the Hebrew Scriptures and there are logical reasons for their differences; but the list in Revelation corresponds to none of them (see Gn 35:22-26; 46:8-27; Ex 1:2-4; Nb 1:4-15; 13:4-16). My own speculation for the mention of Levi is that the scene involves worship and liturgy; two responsibilities belonging to the tribe of Levi. Manasseh is added while Ephraim is left out, probably because Joseph the father of Ephraim is mentioned.

Should we identify the twelve tribes with the Jews or the synagogue? Undoubtedly, John of Patmos was a Christian Jew and saw in the faithful members of the twelve tribes the true and renewed Israel. They are not to be excluded from the presence of God and the Lamb. Whether they are Jews, Jewish-Christians, the Christian Church inclusive of Jews and Christians, or the martyrs of the Church is what the exegetes struggle with. Once again, by including all of these interpretations we are closer to what the visionary intends.

The Multitude from Every Nation (Rv 7:9-17)

Besides the election and charism of being chosen, the tribes of Israel had the message of bringing God to all the nations. Universalism was part of the message of Isaiah and Jeremiah. Thus, in this second scene, the nations are also victorious over evil by the blood of the Lamb and by their faithful worship of God.

Chapter seven of Revelation is an interlude between the sixth seal and the final seventh seal. The section of the multitude from every nation is the climax of this final seal, once again through the prophetic or anticipated victory of the Lamb and the fidelity of all believers. There is great hope for such an innumerable multitude who also will come to witness to the truth and victory of the Lamb. Both soteriology (salvation history) and eschatology are in this scene.

The multitude rings out in chorus with a victory song similar to what Miriam sang in the Exodus event. Praise and glory are given to God and to the Lamb who stands victorious at the right of the throne of God. The inner court of God composed of the angels, the elders, and the four living creatures join in the victory chant which contains the fullness of worship expressed in seven distinct phases: blessing, glory and wisdom, and thanksgiving, honor, power and might be to our God forever and ever! Amen! These sevenfold dimensions of worship are indicative of our own liturgical celebration of God's presence in word and sacrament within the Church.

Throughout this chapter we are immersed in a background flowing from the Exodus event. The ordeals are similar to the plagues; the mark on the forehead is the sign which protects the faithful just as the blood of the Paschal Lamb had protected the dwellings of the Israelites.

This last vision is given an interpretation by one of the elders who explains why both the twelve tribes and the infinite number of peoples are saved and are victorious. Those who have the palm of victory and the white robes of righteousness have come through the great tribulation. They are now in the presence of God, living and worshiping in the heavenly realm. Just as the servants in the temple worshiped God day and night, these tribes and nations incessantly praise God. All forms of suffering and oppression have vanished. They neither hunger nor thirst, they are not oppressed by scorching heat, for the Lamb at the center of the throne is now their leader and shepherd who guides them to waters of eternal life and who wipes every tear from their eyes.

The image of Jesus as Messiah was indicated by Judah leading the list of the tribes. Now the image of Jesus as shepherd leads all to enjoy the waters of eternity amidst the glorious choir of angels, elders, apostles and martyrs. And let us not forget the mysterious four living creatures whom we can call the cherubim.

There is also the only parallel to the greatest christological statement in the New Testament found in Jn 1:14: "And the Word became flesh and pitched his tent among us, and we have seen his glory, the glory as of a father's only son, full of grace and truth." In Revelation 7:15c the parallel reads "and the one seated upon the throne (God) will spread his tent over them" (*skenôsei ep' autous*).

Food for the Journey:

Deuteronomy 7:6,8-9

> [6]For you are a people holy to the Lord your God; the Lord your God has chosen you out of all the peoples on earth to be his people, his treasured possession. [8]It was because the Lord loved you and kept the oath that he swore to your ancestors, that the Lord has brought you out with a mighty hand, and redeemed you from the house of slavery, from the hand of Pharaoh king of Egypt. [9]Know therefore that the Lord your God is God, the faithful God who maintains covenant loyalty with those who love him and keep his commandments, to a thousand generations.

CHAPTER FOUR

THE SEVEN TRUMPETS
(Rv 8-11)

Revelation 8:1-13

[1]When the Lamb opened the seventh seal, there was silence in heaven for about half an hour. [2]And I saw the seven angels who stand before God, and seven trumpets were given to them.

[3]Another angel with a golden censer came and stood at the altar; he was given a great quantity of incense to offer with the prayers of all the saints on the golden altar that is before the throne. [4]And the smoke of the incense, with the prayers of the saints, rose before God from the hand of the angel. [5]Then the angel took the censer and filled it with fire from the altar and threw it on the earth; and there were peals of thunder, rumblings, flashes of lightning, and an earthquake.

[6]Now the seven angels who had the seven trumpets made ready to blow them.

[7]The first angel blew his trumpet, and there came hail and fire, mixed with blood, and they were hurled to the earth; and a third of the earth was burned up, and a third of the trees were burned up, and all green grass was burned up.

[8]The second angel blew his trumpet, and something like a great mountain, burning with fire, was thrown into the sea. [9]A third of the sea became blood, a third of the living creatures in the sea died, and a third of the ships were destroyed.

[10]The third angel blew his trumpet, and a great star fell from

heaven, blazing like a torch, and it fell on a third of the rivers and on the springs of water. [11]The name of the star is Wormwood. A third of the waters became wormwood, and many died from the water, because it was made bitter.

[12]The fourth angel blew his trumpet, and a third of the sun was struck, and a third of the moon, and a third of the stars, so that a third of their light was darkened; a third of the day was kept from shining, and likewise the night.

[13]Then I looked, and I heard an eagle crying with a loud voice as it flew in midheaven, "Woe, woe, woe to the inhabitants of the earth, at the blasts of the other trumpets that the three angels are about to blow!"

John of Patmos speaks:

Silence! I felt I was back in the church at Ephesus and enjoyed silent meditation with the other worshipers. The contemplative half-hour was welcomed after the unsealing of the seventh seal. As I looked toward the throne the seven angels were posed with seven trumpets ready to sound them. But first a great cloud of incense wafted over me and one of the other angels threw his censer to the earth with a paean of thunder, lightning and noise.

Each of the seven angels took a turn at sounding a trumpet. What followed seemed to be a reenactment of the great plagues that had invaded Pharaoh's Egypt and its people. Hail, fire and conflagration follow from the first trumpet; then the second trumpet turned the sea into a bloody red color. Poison like wormwood fell on the earth as the third trumpet blared; then the sun, moon and stars were disturbed by one third of their force and number. An eagle screeched out three woes which would come from the three remaining trumpet blasts.

The first woe was horrendous and came from the lower regions of the earth, the abyss where Abbadon (Apollyon) reigns. Warriors like scorpions which were armed to the teeth came out amidst smoke and flames and tormented and stung with their bites the people who had not been signed with God's seal upon their forehead. I was again remembering the Exodus event and how only those whose door posts were signed with the blood of the Passover Lamb were saved from the plagues. Ugh! this was only the first of three woes. Could I endure two more?

The sixth angel blew his trumpet and the four angels who held back the waters of the Euphrates released the waters and they invaded the earth killing a third of its inhabitants. I remembered how much this resembled the great Parthian bowmen whom the Romans feared; but these angels were in charge of a greater cavalry with red, blue, and sulfur yellow breastplates.

They slaughtered those who were unrepentant and those who were idolaters. What a bloody mess this was!

A mighty angel descended from heaven, so colossal that his right foot was on the sea and his left foot on the land. He had a small scroll in his hand which I was told to eat. It was bitter to the stomach but sweet in my mouth. This was a sign that I was to prophesy. Time was running short and the seventh trumpet was to be sounded which would mean God's hidden purpose will have been accomplished. I remembered Ezekiel's similar experience and I winced at what this all meant for me.

The next thing I was to do was to measure the temple of God and the altar and those within the temple. I was told not to measure the outer court where the Romans will trample and desecrate the holy city for forty-two months. Two witnesses dressed in sackcloth would prophesy, but be killed by the beast. Their corpses would lie in the street for three and a half days, but afterward they would rise and ascend into heaven, while an earthquake would kill seven thousand. This would be the second woe.

Then the seventh angel blew his trumpet and the praise and adoration of God was resumed by all in the heavenly court. The nations were soon to be judged and the chorus chanted more thanks to God, for the oppressors were to be destroyed and God's servants rewarded.

All of a sudden God's sanctuary was opened and I saw the ark of the covenant and a theophany of lightning, thunder, and heavy hail.

COMMENTARY

The Seven Angels and the Golden Censer (Rv 8:1-13)

For the sake of convenience I have followed the chapters as they are presented in the New Testament. We know that this is an artificial division that often breaks up the continuity of the narrative. For example, Aune, a leading exegete on Revelation, would see the seventh seal and the first six trumpets (8:1-11:14) forming a unit; in a more focused division the unit could be treated as the seventh seal (8:1) and the vision of the first six trumpets (8:2-9:21).

The seventh seal is opened by the Lamb and for a half hour silence occurs in the heavens. As a literary device this produces a dramatic effect showing that the entire eschatological plan of God is now being revealed, for the seventh seal opens the entire message of Revelation. The silence is also a sign of theological importance. Habakkuk and Zechariah illustrate this:

> "But the Lord is in his holy temple; let all the earth keep silence before him!" (Hab 2:20) and "Be silent, all people, before the Lord; for he has roused himself from his holy dwelling" (Zc 2:13).

Silence indicates a solemn prelude to what is about to happen. The throne visions are coming to an end, the catastrophes which follow are initiated by the seven angels with the corresponding trumpet blare, each of which announces the calamity. Heaven and earth are in conflict, but the heavenly powers are thoroughly in charge.

We see the seven angels standing before the throne of God, being given seven trumpets. These may be what are called archangels in tradition. Three are mentioned in the Scriptures: Michael, Gabriel, Raphael; while four come from extra-biblical sources: Uriel, Raguel, Sariel, and Remiel (I Enoch 20).

An angel initiates the action by filling a golden censer with embers; the fragrant aroma from the embers represents the prayers of those who have been martyred and who are near or under the golden altar in heaven. Their prayers are effective for the wrath of God is about to ensue after each angel blows a trumpet. Verses 3-5 are bound up with terms proper to the temple worship: censer, altar, incense, prayer, hands, holy ones, and the throne of God. The liturgical dimension of Revelation is one of its positive qualities. Often throughout the narrative, a liturgical scene will calm the tremendous violence and destruction that unfolds in the eschatological portrayal of the book. It is noteworthy that the angels are the ones who present the prayers of the saints (*hagioi*) before God (v. 4c). Once the angel casts the censer to earth, the patterned cosmic disturbances appear: thunder, rumblings, lightning and an earthquake. We have already referred to the earthquake that disturbed twelve cities in the area of the seven churches; in Italy another great eruption at Vesuvius took place in 79 C.E. which may have prompted verse 8 of this section. In three of the four references to cosmic disturbances, an earthquake is included (see Rv 8:56; 11:19c: 16:18-21).

Besides the pattern of cosmic disturbance, the visionary also has the same division of 4+3 that he used in relating to us the story regarding the seven seals. The angels with their trumpets follow that same 4+3 arrangement.

The background from the book of Exodus is probably the source for the seven plagues. Even though there are ten plagues listed in the Exodus saga, there is evidence in the Yahwist tradition or source and in the Psalms which would support the idea of just seven plagues (Ps 78:43-52; Ps 105:27-36; Am 4:6-13). The ten plagues in Exodus demonstrate the characteristics of the Priestly (P) tradition (Ex 7:8-13:16).

These plagues are a divine punishment while the prayers of the saints who have been martyred are the reason for the plagues. Their prayers may be a cry for justice and a thanksgiving for deliverance; let us not exclude that they are also wrathful prayers. The all too human reaction for vengeance not only is common to the Hebrew Scriptures but to the Christian Scriptures as well!

Verse 6 is a transitional verse which lines up the seven angels and announces that they are about to sound their trumpets, each one in succession. The plagues then will fall upon the earth and its inhabitants.

With the first angel sounding the trumpet, the plagues of hail and fire are thrown down to earth; the destruction leaves only two-thirds of the earth unburned, and two-thirds of the trees. All green grass, however, is burned. The one-third is a typical part of prophetic language (Ezk 5:12-13; Rv 12:4). This first plague is similar to the seventh in Ex 9:25: "The hail struck down everything that was in the open field throughout all the land of Egypt, both human and animal; the hail also struck down all the plants of the fields, and shattered every tree in the field."

Likewise the second plague in Revelation is similar to the first plague in Ex 7:20-21: "...and all the water was turned into blood, and the fish in the river died" (Ex 7:20c-21a).

These parallels in the plagues are loosely connected to those mentioned in Exodus; a striking difference is the universality of the calamity in Revelation to the restricted local situation in Ex 7-14.

The angels are using phenomena that are associated with the threefold tier concept of the creation story in Genesis. Notice how all calamities emanate from the height of heaven or from light: hail and fire from the heavens, a great mountain burning with fire, a star blazing like a torch, the sun, moon and stars, etc. It seems like the heavens are "getting even" with the earth for persecuting the holy ones of God.

The third angel brings with the sound of the trumpet a great star or meteorite which falls into the waters and poisons them with its bitter aftermath named "Wormwood." Here many die from this bitterness. This is the first time that the plague has destroyed humans. This plague is also similar to the first plague in Ex 7:14-25.

There is a great similarity in the scenes of the trumpets to those of the seals. Basically it is the same revelation of what is to happen, but here it is progressively worse from one-fourth to one-third. The series started with the message of salvation and judgment upon the churches. It passes now into the world or earth in the next phase of the same vision; now with the trumpets it is the entire cosmos that is involved in the salvation and judgment of God. Salvation for those around the throne; judgment upon the universe.

The fourth angel's trumpet eclipses the sun by one-third; the same is true for the moon and the stars. This resembles the ninth plague of Ex 10:21: "So Moses stretched out his hand toward heaven, and there was dense darkness in the land of Egypt for three days."

The visionary sees and hears an eagle flying in mid-heaven and squawking out with a loud sound "Woe! Woe! Woe!" signaling that three more devastating episodes are to be expected from the final triad of trumpet-bearing angels. The eagle as a symbol represents God. It also was the symbol for the Roman army which had inflicted punishment and death upon many nations and also upon the righteous.

Food for the Journey:

Psalm 141:1,2

[1]I call upon you, O Lord; come quickly to me; give ear to my voice when I call to you. [2]Let my prayer be counted as incense before you, and the lifting up of my hands as an evening sacrifice.

Revelation 9:1-21

[1]And the fifth angel blew his trumpet, and I saw a star that had fallen from heaven to earth, and he was given the key to the shaft of the bottomless pit; [2]he opened the shaft of the bottomless pit, and from the shaft rose smoke like the smoke of a great furnace, and the sun and the air were darkened with the smoke from the shaft. [3]Then from the smoke came locusts on the earth, and they were given authority like the authority of scorpions of the earth. [4]They were told not to damage the grass of the earth or any green

growth or any tree, but only those people who do not have the seal of God on their foreheads. [5]They were allowed to torture them for five months, but not to kill them, and their torture was like the torture of a scorpion when it stings someone. [6]And in those days people will seek death but will not find it; they will long to die, but death will flee from them.

[7]In appearance the locusts were like horses equipped for battle. On their heads were what looked like crowns of gold; their faces were like human faces, [8]their hair like women's hair, and their teeth like lions' teeth; [9]they had scales like iron breastplates, and the noise of their wings was like the noise of many chariots with horses rushing into battle. [10]They have tails like scorpions, with stingers, and in their tails is their power to harm people for five months. [11]They have as king over them the angel of the bottomless pit; his name in Hebrew is Abaddon, and in Greek he is called Apollyon.

[12]The first woe has passed. There are still two woes to come.

[13]Then the sixth angel blew his trumpet, and I heard a voice from the four horns of the golden altar before God, [14]saying to the sixth angel who had the trumpet, "Release the four angels who are bound at the great river Euphrates." [15]So the four angels were released, who had been held ready for the hour, the day, the month, and the year, to kill a third of humankind. [16]The number of the troops of cavalry was two hundred million; I heard their number. [17]And this was how I saw the horses in my vision: the riders wore breastplates the color of fire and of sapphire and of sulfur; the heads of the horses were like lions' heads, and fire and smoke and sulfur came out of their mouths. [18]By these three plagues a third of humankind was killed, by the fire and smoke and sulfur coming out of their mouths. [19]For the power of the horses is in their mouths and in their tails; their tails are like serpents, having heads; and with them they inflict harm.

[20]The rest of humankind, who were not killed by these plagues, did not repent of the works of their hands or give up worshiping demons and idols of gold and silver and bronze and stone and wood, which cannot see or hear or walk. [21]And they did not repent of their murders or their sorceries or their fornication or their thefts.

COMMENTARY

The fifth and sixth trumpets (Rv 9:1-21)

The description taken from the vision of John of Patmos for the fifth and sixth angel and the corresponding blare of their trumpets offers much greater detail for the effectiveness of the plagues and punishment inflicted on humanity. It could be the case, that once the underworld's shaft is open, worse calamities proceed from the realm of the demons and their leader.

The first twelve lines are given to this sixth scene which is also the first of the woes. The next pericope (Rv 9:13-21), the woes, is a description of the sixth angel's trumpet and the havoc caused on earth among humans.

The fifth trumpet (Rv 9:1-12)

The star that falls to the earth and opens the shaft of the underworld is most likely an angelic being having great power. Angels were frequently symbolized by stars in Jewish literature. In the apocryphal Sibylline Oracles the following parallel symbolism helps us understand this association: "A great star will come from heaven to the wondrous sea and will burn the deep sea and Babylon itself and the land of Italy, because of which many holy faithful Hebrews and a true people perished" (Aune, p. 525, Vol. 52b and Charlesworth, OTP2:397).

In the book of Revelation the abyss or boundless depths is the abode of the demons and Satan. In the form of locusts that could be so numerous as to darken the skies, the demons leave their chaotic underworld following their leader Abbadon or Apollyon. The Hebrew word Abbadon is used here as a personification of the prince of darkness and death and is connected with the concept of Sheol or Hades. Apollyon is the Greek equivalent of the leader of this underworld. Locusts also recall the eighth plague of Ex 10:12-20. The locust-like creatures are compared to scorpions

which have excruciating pain in their sting; sometimes even caus-
ing death to their victims. Notice that the verbs describing them
are in the passive voice. This indicates that they ultimately have
their power through God who allows them to exist. They would
have no such power on their own. This intimates that God's punishment is wrought through them.

The similarity of what is to be spared, namely, the grass of
the earth, the plants, the trees has already been noticed in chapter 7:2-3. Only those humans who have been marked with the seal
of God on their heads are to be spared.

The number five is used in this scene: it is the fifth trumpet
and the angel and the affliction will last five months. Five symbolizes something for a shorter duration or a number expressing fewer.
Locusts also have a five-month cycle to their lives.

The imagery of the locusts who are as large as a cavalry recalls the Parthians, Rome's dreaded enemy. The Parthian empire
(240 B.C.E.-226 C.E.) had legendary horsemen who were expert
bowsmen. Their horses were prized for their size and were in great
demand as far as China. Their "blood sweating" horses could have
been described in this plague which would annihilate one third of
the Romans. During the last decades of the first century the
Parthians were a constant threat to the Roman Empire. They were
always prepared to cross the Euphrates. Vologesus, a military leader,
did conquer some Roman legions in 62 C.E. The description of
the armor and of the covered heads of these bowmen may account
for the vivid and horrific images of the locusts. The sting of a scorpion may refer to their arrows afflicting the enemy.

The visionary who is so imbued with the prophetic message
of the Hebrew Scriptures could also have been influenced by Joel
and Amos in describing the cavalry of locusts: "...the day of the
Lord is coming, it is near — a day of darkness and gloom, a day of
clouds and thick darkness! ... a great and powerful army comes.

"They have the appearance of horses, and like war-horses they
charge. As with the rumbling of chariots, they leap on the tops of
mountains, like the crackling flame of fire, devouring the stubble,

like a powerful army drawn up for battle" (Jl 2:1c-5) also (Na 3:15-17).

The writer pauses and declares the first woe is past; two more woes are to follow after this (Rv 9:12).

The sixth angel (Rv 9:13-21)

The sixth angel unleashes the four angels who are bound up at the Euphrates River. This plague brings about the death of one-third of the human race. The bind/release motif suggests the demons (bad angels) who lead the cavalry described in lurid colors and in outlandish numbers of millions upon millions. Sodom and Gomorrah are brought to mind with the mention of the smoke and sulfur coming out of the horses' mouths.

Dramatically the seer sadly comments that the rest of humankind does not repent (*metanôiesan*); they continue their idolatrous worship of false gods made of gold, silver, bronze and wood. Could the seer be referring to the sin of worshiping wealth and merchandise while neglecting to worship God the Creator? The theme of not repenting is characteristic of the Exodus plagues (Ex 7:13,22; 8:15) and also summarizes the motif in this section of Revelation. There is also a remarkable similarity to breaking the fifth, sixth, and seventh commandments in verse 21. Aune provides an excellent synoptic companion to these three vices in Rv 9:20-21, Rv 21:8, and Rv 22:15. "The parallels between Exodus 7:8-13:16 (the ten Exodus plagues) and Revelation 8:1-11:19 and 15:1-16:21 indicate that Exodus provided the model for the author's vision of the eschatological punishments inflicted by God on the unbelieving inhabitants of the world" (Aune, *Rev. Vol. 52B*, p. 546).

The sevenfold trumpet blare signified an all out war — a "world war," while the trumpet sound in Roman culture meant a disrupture between the gods and humans.

Once again, our knowledge of the Hebrew Scriptures helps us to understand the symbolism of Revelation.

Food for the Journey:

Psalm 135:15-18

[15]The idols of the nations are silver and gold, the work of human hands. [16]They have mouths, but they do not speak; they have eyes, but they do not see; [17]they have ears, but they do not hear, and there is no breath in their mouths. [18]Those who make them and all who trust them shall become like them.

Revelation 10:1-11

[1]And I saw another mighty angel coming down from heaven, wrapped in a cloud, with a rainbow over his head; his face was like the sun, and his legs like pillars of fire. [2]He held a little scroll open in his hand. Setting his right foot on the sea and his left foot on the land, [3]he gave a great shout, like a lion roaring. And when he shouted, the seven thunders sounded. [4]And when the seven thunders had sounded, I was about to write, but I heard a voice from heaven saying, "Seal up what the seven thunders have said, and do not write it down." [5]Then the angel whom I saw standing on the sea and the land raised his right hand to heaven [6]and swore by him who lives forever and ever, who created heaven and what is in it, the earth and what is in it, and the sea and what is in it: "There will be no more delay, [7]but in the days when the seventh angel is to blow his trumpet, the mystery of God will be fulfilled, as he announced to his servants the prophets."

[8]Then the voice that I had heard from heaven spoke to me again, saying, "Go, take the scroll that is open in the hand of the angel who is standing on the sea and on the land." [9]So I went to the angel and told him to give me the little scroll; and he said to me, "Take it, and eat; it will be bitter to your stomach, but sweet as honey in your mouth." [10]So I took the little scroll from the hand of the angel and ate it; it was sweet as honey in my mouth, but when I had eaten it, my stomach was made bitter.

[11]Then they said to me, "You must prophesy again about many peoples and nations and languages and kings."

COMMENTARY

The Magnificent Angel and the Little Scroll (Rv 10:1-11)

Homer could not have crafted a better description of this angel and its cosmic grandeur. The heavens are its boundary while clouds wrap around it and the sun and a rainbow crown the angel. This angel holds a small scroll in its hands, while its right foot gleaming with burnished fire rests on the sea and its left foot on the land. The powerful angel bellows like a lion and his cry resonates as an echo from the seven thunders who reveal something to the seer. John of Patmos has an urge to write it down, but is told not to write. The seer is being prepared to be a prophet. His confirmation as a prophet will follow.

Our monumental angel then swears by the Creator of heaven and earth and all that is in it that there will be no more delay. One would expect that it is the seventh angel ready to sound the seventh trumpet. Not so, for this angel is the announcer of God's secret for the final unfolding of history through the prophetic messages of God's servants, the prophets. Our own John of Patmos is being called to share in the call of prophecy; only then will the fulfillment of the mystery of God be accomplished.

The scene displays an interruption between the sounding of the sixth trumpet and the seventh (9:13 and 11:15). This same pattern was seen between the sixth and the seventh seal. It seems that it is part of John's style to help the reader experience a comforting moment, a contemplative hour, so to speak, before hearing of further calamities upon the inhabitants of the earth. This is a welcome pause in which the power of God's agents and the presence of the *Pantocrator* (the Almighty) is recalled. The mystery is that the Messiah (Jesus Christ) will reign forever and that all of God's creatures are to respond in profound adoration and worship. These glimpses into the purpose of the book of Revelation enable us moderns to realize this is at the heart of what the book is all about.

In personally experiencing how often the liturgical readings of the hours recall phrases and prayers from Revelation, one realizes how helpful such an insight is for praising and worshiping God with expressions from the Hebrew Scriptures like "Amen! Alleluia!" "Worship the one who was, who is, and who will be for ages unto ages. Amen!"

The connective imagery in chapter ten is seen in its repetition. One has the feeling that here is where the Semitic style of our author comes out so well in patterns of parallel imagery and repetitiveness. It is not boring to hear about this angel whose right foot is on the sea and its left foot on the land; both land and sea are constantly being mentioned throughout Revelation. Like the favorite themes of a musical masterpiece, John of Patmos keeps bringing them back through his use of symbolism in numbers and in favorite theological events like the creation of the heavens and earth; the contrasts of peace and war; the exodus song of victory together with the woeful plagues. All this imagery moves in and out, up and down, almost in a rhyme and rhythm.

It is with the seventh trumpet that the mystery of God will be revealed through the prophets of the past, but also, as we shall see, through the call of a latter day saint and prophet, John of Patmos. John is called to be a prophet.

Though we already know that the seer has been called to prophesy about what he has seen, in this part of his vision the call to prophesy again (v. 11) is within the context of a prophetic vocation described in a manner similar to the call of Ezekiel (Ezk 2:8-3:3):

> But you, mortal, hear what I say to you; do not be rebellious like that rebellious house; open your mouth and eat what I give you." I looked, and a hand was stretched out to me, and a written scroll was in it. He spread it before me; it had writing on the front and on the back, and written on it were words of lamentation and mourning and woe. He said to me, "O mortal, eat what is offered to you; eat this scroll, and go, speak to the house of Israel." So I opened my mouth, and

he gave me the scroll to eat. He said to me, "Mortal, eat this scroll that I give you and fill your stomach with it." Then I ate it and in my mouth it was as sweet as honey.

Such oral imagery is common to the prophetic call of the great prophets. Isaiah's mouth is purified with a burning ember (Is 6:6-7); Jeremiah's mouth is touched by the Lord (Jr 1:9). We can see how both the experience of John of Patmos and its similarity to Ezekiel's call help us to appreciate how much this book of Revelation is dependent upon the Hebrew prophetic literature. Some scholars say there are between 200 to 500 allusions to the Old Testament. The language, imagery, and themes need not be sought in the mythology outside the Bible, they merely confirm and parallel what the word of God has said through the prophets. In John of Patmos we are dealing with a Jewish Christian who is immersed in his own *Torah* and *Nebiim* (Prophets).

John, to our amazement, reaches out and politely asks for the scroll from this colossal angel. No questions asked! He tells the seer to eat the little scroll which will sour his stomach but be sweet as honey in his mouth. The event happens. The prophet is born; he will prophesy for the rest of his revelational experience.

John has been commissioned to prophesy over "against the peoples and nations and languages and kings." This fourfold description occurs seven times within Revelation (5:9; 7:9; 10:11; 11:9; 13:7; 14:6; 17:15). It is found in a similar way in Daniel, the only authentic apocalyptic work of the Hebrew Bible (see Dn 3:4, 7:29; 5:19; 6:25; 7:14). Once again we are touching the ultimate sources of the book of Revelation, namely, the Hebrew Scriptures.

Patrick Sena summarizes this section succinctly: "The little scroll should be identified with the New Testament which Christ has given us. Unlike the seven-sealed scroll which could only have fulfillment with the coming of Christ (i.e., the O.T.), the little scroll's message is clear to those who will accept it. John has to take it himself; he has to digest it; the message is sweet since it is Jesus Christ. Nevertheless, when he preaches, bitterness will come to him, because those to whom he preaches will not readily accept the message. It is the role of the preacher of the Gospel; the sweetness will get him through the bitterness" (P.J. Sena, C.PP.S., *The Apocalypse: Biblical Revelation Explained*, Alba House, New York, 1985, p. 66).

Food for the Journey:

Ezekiel 2:8-9; 3:1-4

> [8]"But you, mortal, hear what I say to you; do not be rebellious like that rebellious house; open your mouth and eat what I give you." [9]I looked, and a hand was stretched out to me, and a written scroll was in it.
>
> [3:1]He said to me, "O mortal, eat what is offered to you; eat this scroll, and go, speak to the house of Israel." [2]So I opened my mouth, and he gave me the scroll to eat. [3]He said to me, "Mortal, eat this scroll that I give you and fill your stomach with it." Then I ate it; and in my mouth it was as sweet as honey. [4]He said to me: "Mortal, go to the house of Israel and speak my very words to them."

Revelation 11:1-19

> [1]Then I was given a measuring rod like a staff, and I was told, "Come and measure the temple of God and the altar and those who worship there, [2]but do not measure the court outside the temple; leave that out, for it is given over to the nations, and they will trample over the holy city for forty-two months. [3]And I will grant my two witnesses authority to prophesy for one thousand two hundred sixty days, wearing sackcloth."
>
> [4]These are the two olive trees and the two lampstands that stand before the Lord of the earth. [5]And if anyone wants to harm them, fire pours from their mouth and consumes their foes; anyone who wants to harm them must be killed in this manner. [6]They have authority to shut the sky, so that no rain may fall during the days of their prophesying, and they have authority over the wa-

ters to turn them into blood, and to strike the earth with every kind of plague, as often as they desire.

[7]When they have finished their testimony, the beast that comes up from the bottomless pit will make war on them and conquer them and kill them, [8]and their dead bodies will lie in the street of the great city that is prophetically called Sodom and Egypt, where also their Lord was crucified. [9]For three and a half days members of the peoples and tribes and languages and nations will gaze at their dead bodies and refuse to let them be placed in a tomb; [10]and the inhabitants of the earth will gloat over them and celebrate and exchange presents, because these two prophets had been a torment to the inhabitants of the earth.

[11]But after the three and a half days, the breath of life from God entered them, and they stood on their feet, and those who saw them were terrified. [12]Then they heard a loud voice from heaven saying to them, "Come up here!" And they went up to heaven in a cloud while their enemies watched them. [13]At that moment there was a great earthquake, and a tenth of the city fell; seven thousand people were killed in the earthquake, and the rest were terrified and gave glory to the God of heaven.

[14]The second woe has passed. The third woe is coming very soon.

[15]Then the seventh angel blew his trumpet, and there were loud voices in heaven, saying, "The kingdom of the world has become the kingdom of our Lord and of his Messiah, and he will reign forever and ever."

[16]Then the twenty-four elders who sit on their thrones before God fell on their faces and worshiped God, [17]singing,

> "We give you thanks, Lord God Almighty,
> who are and who were,
> for you have taken your great power
> and begun to reign.
> [18]The nations raged,
> but your wrath has come,
> and the time for judging the dead,
> for rewarding your servants, the prophets

and saints and all who fear your name,
both small and great,
and for destroying those who destroy the earth."

[19]Then God's temple in heaven was opened, and the ark of
his covenant was seen within his temple; and there were flashes
of lightning, rumblings, peals of thunder, an earthquake, and
heavy hail.

COMMENTARY

The Measuring of the Temple and the Two Witnesses (Rv 11)

This chapter is intriguing. The first unit may be divided into
(1) the measuring of the temple by John (11:1-2); (2) the death
and resurrection of two witnesses (*martyres*) (11:3-13); a transitional verse (v. 14) that leads us into the conclusion of chapter
11; and finally the seventh trumpet (11:15-18). It is best to con-
sider verse 19 as part of the extraordinary vision of the woman
clothed with the sun in chapter 12.

The Measuring of the Temple (Rv 11:1-2)

There is an unknown speaker who addresses John to measure
the temple which is in Jerusalem. The outer court where Gentiles
were permitted is not to be measured. Scholars think that this section of Revelation may be one of the oldest, probably issuing from
a source written at the time of the destruction of the temple by
the Romans in 70 C.E. The contextual symbolism of the entire
chapter centers on Jerusalem and the heart and soul of Jewish pi-
ety, the temple. Once again, this is a parallel image of the temple
being measured by Ezekiel, the prophet upon whom our author re-
lies. In Ezekiel the reed of measurement tips us toward seeing such
a similarity in the opening verse of this section:

"When he brought me there, a man was there whose appearance shone like bronze, with a linen cord and a measuring reed in his hand; and he was standing in the gateway." (Ezk 40:3)

The development of the narrative of Ezekiel concerning the measurement and vision of the new temple comprises chapters 40-42. This description helps us understand what the seer is now experiencing.

Surprisingly, John never actually measures the temple even though he has constantly followed all of the other commands or heavenly voices. The measuring is a symbolic prophetic action which is paradoxical for it can mean preservation and/or destruction. The unknown voice certainly comes from God or an agent of God giving another divine imperative: "Get up!" Measuring and counting are implied in the verb since there is a focus on the inner court that will continue through the appearance of the Ark of the Covenant. This idea seems to symbolically speak of preservation rather than destruction.

Those in the inner court who are measured (numbered) are the faithful people of God and they will be protected. The outsiders in the adjacent court are not so fortunate. They are not measured or counted among the elect. Remember that those who worship God are the faithful ones and are protected by God despite the tribulations and persecution they have suffered.

With chapter eleven our prophet and visionary now begins to take on an active prophetic role. He is being prepared for the seventh angel's trumpet announcement and for the final and climactic scenes of struggle between those who are authentic worshipers and those who are lured by the symbols of evil and the agents of Satan.

The symbolism of numbers has become familiar to us. Most of the references to eschatological events in Revelation are taken from the numerical equivalents in Daniel, another Jewish apocalyptic source that has influenced the seer from Patmos. Daniel has the same forty-two months or one thousand and sixty days. Likewise in Rv 11:9 there is a reference to three and a half days, Daniel's equivalent is a time, two times and a half time (see Dn 7:25 and 12:7).

In summary, verse one refers to the holy people of God, true worshipers; verse two, however, indicates those outside who are not measured. This court will be trampled upon for 42 months, and probably refers to the Roman destruction which will take place in the earthly notion of the temple.

The two witnesses: Rv 11:3-13

The Apocalypse is filled with multiple forms of symbolism. In our present unit the two witnesses are couched in symbolic language. All is centered on their powerful witness to the peoples who are connected with Jerusalem and to those people who are familiar with the power-filled feats of the Elijah traditions and the Exodus plagues conducted by Moses, the mediator between God and the Israelites. Symbols, however, are quite fluid and plastic. They conjure up many interpretive possibilities. For example, scholars see in the two witnesses multiple dyads like: messianic figures as a priestly messiah of Aaron and a Davidic king-like Messiah; Moses and Elijah; Enoch and Elijah; Elijah and Jeremiah. Other exegetes favor a Peter and Paul interpretation; or Stephen and James the Just; John the Baptist and Jesus; James the Just and James the son of Zebedee; or the high priests Ananias and Joshua. Still other interpreters go completely into a symbolic meaning: the Old Testament and the New Testament; or Christian preachers and teachers; the spiritual values of Israel continued in the Church; the Word of God and the testimony of Jesus. (See Aune, Vol. 52B, pp. 598-603 for a detailed account of all of the above interpretations).

Aune favors, as do most scholars, the persons of Elijah and Moses. He ends the discussion with the following helpful insight: "The present form of the narrative has a symbolic character and should not be taken as a sequence of events that the author expected would take place literally. With regard to the symbolic significance of the two witnesses, it is relatively clear that they represent the witnesses of the people of God in a godless world and that they, like their Lord, will ultimately triumph over suffering and death" (Aune, Vol. 52B, p. 603).

The two great events of Judaism and Christianity lie in the background of this section. For Judaism the Exodus signifying liberation for God's people from their afflictions is seen through the mention of the plagues. Certainly, for Christianity the Paschal Mystery of Jesus is implied through verse 8: "Their bodies will lie in the public square of the great city, which is called, prophetically, 'Sodom' and 'Egypt,' where their Lord was crucified" (Aune's translation). The witnesses' resurrection is undoubtedly modeled on that of Jesus on the third day. Almost every exegete sees a Christian interpretation in verse 8 because of the mention of Jesus' death. The rest of the pericope could have been a Jewish narrative wherein only one witness was given. Here in Revelation it has been retouched into two witnesses who continue being addressed and described by other symbols used by the visionary. They are compared to two olive trees and two lampstands. The olive tree symbolism comes from the prophet Zechariah 4:3 (a favorite source of Revelation); the two menorahs or lampstands also spring from Zechariah 4:2-3,11. The readers are familiar with the Fourth Gospel naming John as a lamp (Jn 1:6 and Jn 5:35; similarly 2 P 1:19).

These two witnesses in ascetical dress disturb the status quo of power, politics, and opulence in the worldly symbolism of Sodom and Egypt; the death of the Lord also implies the secular dimension of Jerusalem under the thumb of Rome.

In verse 14 the reader discovers that two woes are over; now a third woe is predicted, but never occurs in the rest of the Apocalypse. Verse 14 is a transitional verse which summarizes what has taken place and leads the reader to the seventh angel with a trumpet.

The Seventh Trumpet (Rv 11:15-18)

The trumpets of the angels commenced in Rv 8:1-9:21, then two separate units were seen in Rv 10:1-11 and 11:1-14. Here, finally, the seventh trumpet blares, but we have a period of contemplation before the heavenly throne. The victory hymn of God's court is sung and a prayer of thanksgiving is offered by the 24 elders who prostrate themselves before the throne and presence of God. Our visionary takes every opportunity to remind us that God alone is worthy to be worshiped.

By way of a personal note, there is a beautiful arboretum within walking distance of my Marianist community. It is named Woodland and is also a cemetery. As you enter the Mausoleum close to the entrance gates, there is a magnificent stained glass window that captures this scene from the Apocalypse. I have taken classes of students from the University of Dayton and the International Marian Research Institute to view the window. I try to have an artist with me to explain the symbols and colors. I also play Handel's Hallelujah Chorus, which is inspired by Rv 11:15; 19:6 and 19:16. In the center is Christ in royal robes and crowned with a splendid regal crown. The 24 elders are vividly portrayed with an air of reverent adoration: the four living creatures are from left to right at the bottom of the framework. The beautiful deep reds, blues and golden hues come through with the surrounding whites. Correctly, the rainbow as described in Revelation is green. Exuberant joy, peace, and even victory are evident in this splendid window. This is just what our section is telling us: the rule of the Christ who is both the Lamb of God and the Almighty One (*Pantocrator*) has been inaugurated. The surrounding angels, elders, and living creatures capture the meaning of the Communion of Saints. The Apocalypse is a magnificent work of art in literary-symbolic scenes. Artists have realized this and in their works have displayed their own awe and contemplation.

Another personal note will serve as the conclusion for this scene. The recent death of Father Raymond E. Brown, S.S., affected me deeply. I had the honor of being with him on his last visit to

Dayton. It was the occasion of talking about his forthcoming book entitled, *The Death of the Messiah.* I had the good fortune of taking Father Brown to a nearby restaurant for lunch and then for a visit to the Marian Library at the University of Dayton. This is the world's largest Marian research library. Father Brown took the occasion to look up a few references, not missing a moment in his passion for research. Recently, we at the Marian Library had asked him to present a scriptural topic at the forthcoming Mariological Society of America's annual conference. Unfortunately, Father Brown died on August 8, 1998. He was both a friend and a mentor in Scripture for me. I thought you as a reader would enjoy the short paragraph he has in his last book, *An Introduction to the New Testament.* Here is his succinct statement about our passage under consideration: "The seventh trumpet is finally sounded in 11:15-19, signaling that the kingdom of the world has become the kingdom of our Lord and his Christ, to which proclamation there is a hymn of the twenty-four elders/presbyters. This might make us think that the end of the world had come. But there is much more to follow, for the opening of God's temple in heaven to show the Ark of the Covenant (11:19) introduces Part II, even as the open heavenly door in 4:1 introduced Part I" (Brown, *Introduction,* p. 790).

The Ark of the Covenant (Rv 11:19)

Verse 19 of chapter eleven is best seen as a connecting experience of John with the continuing unfolding of the same vision of chapter twelve. Primarily, the woman clothed with the sun is a symbol of the Church; secondarily, in the history of interpretation the same woman is identified with Mary, the Mother of Jesus.

Starting with verse 19 of chapter eleven, we are between the sounding of the seventh trumpet (Rv 11:15-18) and the narrative of the seven bowls (15:1-16:21). The three sections within this continuing development of the conflict between Satan and the woman or between the Roman Empire and the Church are the following: Rv 11:19-12:17; 12:18-13:18; and 14:1-20.

We are at the central revelatory experience of John; the heart of the book of Revelation is now manifested in a struggle between good and evil. The three inaugural visions of this section are of the Ark of the Covenant in heaven linked to the woman in the heavens who is clothed with the sun with her head surrounded by twelve stars and the moon beneath her feet; the scene of the devil or the dragon; and finally the Lamb near the throne of God. Let us start with the Ark of the Covenant which is seen in heaven. Adela Yarbro Collins comments: "Part one concludes with a cryptic but powerful epiphany of the Ark of God's covenant in the heavenly temple — a majestic though indirect manifestation of the presence of God" (*The Apocalypse, New Testament Message 22*, Glazier, Wilmington, Delaware, 1979, p. 75).

The Ark was constructed by Moses and God specified its dimension. The Ark was the earthly throne of God who was seated upon the cherubim. God received the prayers of the Israelites and led them in their expedition. It contained the tablets of the decalogue which was given at Sinai, therefore, it was both the Ark of Testimony and the Ark of the Covenant. Solomon built his temple to house it and it probably remained there until it was destroyed or disappeared. Jeremiah is said to have hidden it in a secret place until God's glory revealed it (2 Mc 2:48). In the New Testament the Ark is only mentioned here and in Heb 9:4. God's mercy and fidelity are being shown through the appearance of the Ark in heaven. The temple doors are open while the surrounding theophany of lightning, rumblings, peals of thunder, an earthquake, and heavy hail dramatize the seer's experience. This recalls the experience of Moses on Mount Sinai. For the seer this may be explained as the aftermath of what happened in chapter eleven which has to do with a spiritual effect of the disastrous destruction of the temple in 70 C.E. and the separation of the synagogue and the Church.

With the appearance of the woman who is primarily a symbol of the Church, the revelation John is experiencing becomes cosmic and universal.

Food for the Journey:

Exodus 37:1-9

¹Bezalel made the Ark of acacia wood; it was two and a half cubits long, a cubit and a half wide, and a cubit and a half high. ²He overlaid it with pure gold inside and outside, and made a molding of gold around it. ³He cast for it four rings of gold for its four feet, two rings on its one side and two rings on its other side. ⁴He made poles of acacia wood, and overlaid them with gold, ⁵and put the poles into the rings on the sides of the Ark, to carry the Ark. ⁶He made a mercy seat of pure gold; two cubits and a half was its length, and a cubit and a half its width. ⁷He made two cherubim of hammered gold; at the two ends of the mercy seat he made them, ⁸one cherub at the one end, and one cherub at the other end; of one piece with the mercy seat he made the cherubim at its two ends. ⁹The cherubim spread out their wings above, overshadowing the mercy seat with their wings. They faced one another; the faces of the cherubim were turned toward the mercy seat.

CHAPTER FIVE

THE WOMAN, A SIGN OF GOD'S GLORY AND VICTORY OVER EVIL
(Rv 12-13)

Revelation 12:1-18

[1]A great portent appeared in heaven: a woman clothed with the sun, with the moon under her feet, and on her head a crown of twelve stars. [2]She was pregnant and was crying out in birth pangs, in the agony of giving birth. [3]Then another portent appeared in heaven: a great red dragon, with seven heads and ten horns, and seven diadems on his heads. [4]His tail swept down a third of the stars of heaven and threw them to the earth. Then the dragon stood before the woman who was about to bear a child, so that he might devour her child as soon as it was born. [5]And she gave birth to a son, a male child, who is to rule all the nations with a rod of iron. But her child was snatched away and taken to God and to his throne; [6]and the woman fled into the wilderness, where she has a place prepared by God, so that there she can be nourished for one thousand two hundred sixty days.

[7]And war broke out in heaven; Michael and his angels fought against the dragon. The dragon and his angels fought back, [8]but they were defeated, and there was no longer any place for them in heaven. [9]The great dragon was thrown down, that ancient serpent, who is called the Devil and Satan, the deceiver of the whole world — he was thrown down to the earth, and his angels were thrown down with him.

¹⁰Then I heard a loud voice in heaven, proclaiming,
"Now have come the salvation and the power
and the kingdom of our God
and the authority of his Messiah,
for the accuser of our comrades has been thrown down,
who accuses them day and night before our God.
¹¹But they have conquered him by the blood of the Lamb
and by the word of their testimony,
for they did not cling to life even in the face of death.
¹²Rejoice then, you heavens
and those who dwell in them!
But woe to the earth and the sea,
for the devil has come down to you
with great wrath,
because he knows that his time is short!"
¹³So when the dragon saw that he had been thrown down to the earth, he pursued the woman who had given birth to the male child. ¹⁴But the woman was given the two wings of the great eagle, so that she could fly from the serpent into the wilderness, to her place where she is nourished for a time, and times, and half a time.

¹⁵Then from his mouth the serpent poured water like a river after the woman, to sweep her away with the flood. ¹⁶But the earth came to the help of the woman; it opened its mouth and swallowed the river that the dragon had poured from his mouth. ¹⁷Then the dragon was angry with the woman, and went off to make war on the rest of her children, those who keep the commandments of God and hold the testimony of Jesus.

¹⁸Then the dragon took his stand on the sand of the seashore.

John of Patmos speaks:

My ecstatic experience is now at its height. I saw a beautiful woman clothed with the sun — a symbol of God's mantle of Love. She was pregnant and ready to give birth. Twelve stars surrounded her head and the moon was beneath her feet. I realized she was the perfect and ideal image for the churches. But, in remembering what I had learned from the disciples of the apostles, I thought of the Mother of Jesus. Let me clarify. I am not the evangelist of a gospel. I am not the beloved disciple to whom Mary was entrusted in a human manner as in a mother and son relationship. In an extended ecclesial way she and he represented the Church. There are memories I have about her and this disciple that stem from the church of Ephesus.

The vision continued and she did give birth to a male child who will rule the nations and shepherd God's people. I could think of no one else but Jesus, the son of Mary, the Messiah. I know he was taken up to heaven and now is reigning with God as the Lamb, the lion of Judah! — pardon the mixed metaphor! — and the root of David.

I blacked out for a moment and later saw Satan the serpent of Genesis, the Devil. He was in combat with the warrior and protector of Israel — the archangel Michael. This adversary (that is what Satan means) lost the battle with Michael ("Who is like to God?" is the meaning of his name). Satan then fits into the vision again for he pursues the woman, that is, he persecutes the Church. It is especially the faithful witnesses to Jesus and those who keep the commandments that this dragon-like figure tries to devour. God, however, like the Exodus event, bears the woman up on eagles' wings (the Law and the Prophets) and brings her, the New Israel, to a safe place in the desert. Both nature and humans rise up to protect her from the fierce dragon. I shall come back to the vision in my next recollection of the great conflict between good and evil which I was privileged to see from my cave.

COMMENTARY

The Woman Clothed with the Sun (Rv 12:1-6)

This pericope is at the center of the book of Revelation and begins the great conflict between the Church and all of its opponents. Satan will lead the attack, but the beast and the Roman

Empire, the greedy and powerful, will continue Satan's onslaught against the people of God.

The magnificent scene of the woman displays the glory of God surrounding her like the sun, and the twelve stars representing either all times and seasons (the Zodiac) or the twelve tribes of Israel continued through the twelve Apostles of the Lamb. The stars are also symbolic of angels. We are again reminded how fluid, malleable, and plastic are the symbols in apocalyptic writings. The woman is in great pain with bringing forth a child. The words used for this excruciating condition are the same as those used for describing the trials, crises, and sufferings of the martyrs or witnesses to the word of God (see also Jn 16:21).

Influenced by some dogmatic statements many Catholic exegetes refrained from applying these pains of childbirth to the Virgin Mary. Other Catholic biblical scholars, however, struggled with the text while applying it to Mary. With more recent developments since Vatican II new avenues are opened to further study of seeing the woman as both the Church and Mary. I prefer to see Mary in a secondary not primary role through the symbol of the woman.

The background and sources for this display of heavenly glory and joy in giving birth stem from the seer experiencing what he knows from the Genesis account of chapter 3:15-16 where there is a struggle of the woman with the serpent, and Genesis 37:9 where Joseph's dream represents his father, mother and brothers seen in the twelve stars. Again, I am not talking about exact equations but about symbolic clusters that are quite fluid and filled with innuendoes or allusions to sources in the Pentateuch/Torah.

The second sign is that of a red dragon which symbolizes Satan. It is the seer himself who gives us the other names of the serpent or dragon: the Devil, Satan, the Deceiver. Throughout the Apocalypse we discover that deception, lying, false, alluring temptations and sensuality are characteristic of what breaks out from Satan. One contemporary psychologist has written a book called *The People of the Lie* (Peck, S., Simon and Schuster, New York, 1983, pp. 182-212). In a chapter which involves the rite of exorcisms of a possessed person, Peck points out how constant confrontation of the demon with truth ultimately effects its expulsion. The constant reiteration of truth whittles away at the horrendous flow of lies and deception coming from the victim's mouth. In the book of Revelation, the narrator constantly reminds the readers that Satan or evil falters and fades when confronted with the truth.

The description of the dragon conjures up the powerful image of the Roman Empire; the ten heads may represent emperors from Nero to Domitian or other governors of Rome. At the same time the symbol of the dragon as the ancient serpent or Satan presents a cosmic conflict with a third of the stars being swept by its tail. Such images merge in the drama presented in symbolic language. This ruthless action of the dragon represents both its power and its wrath against God's creation and against humankind. The seven diadems emphasize its powerful energy. In Genesis 1, God's creative word and spirit sweep over the chaotic waters and life resulted; here the sweep of the dragon produces destruction and chaos.

In Genesis the serpent stood over against the woman telling her to take of the tree of life; here, the dragon stands over against the woman as she is about to bring forth her child. Messianic interpretations can be found not only in the history of the textual tradition and interpretation but also in the reference to Psalm 2:9 which is Messianic and Davidic. There is also a striking Jewish apocryphon on Genesis that highlights and parallels what the seer and the narrator is intending for this messianic context. The Targum for Genesis 3:15 reads:

> I will place enmities between you and the woman between the descendants of your children and her children, and it will come about that when the woman's children observe the precepts of the Torah, they will take aim and crush your head. Whenever, however, they forget the precepts of the Torah, you will be the one who lays the snares and bites their heels. Nevertheless, there is a remedy for them, while for

you there is none. They will find a remedy (or cure) for the heel in the time of the Messiah.

This text is found in a recension of the Targum Pseudo-Jonathan which is substantially the same in the foundational codices and fragments of the Neofiti Targum.

The woman flees to the desert where God has prepared a place for her. She is protected and nourished there for 1260 days. Both the desert theme and the time element are symbolic. The first reading of the text shows that the desert can be a place of refuge or expectation. (1 K 17:2-3; 19:3-4). At Qumran, the community awaited the final eschatological battle (1QM 1:1-3). Aune comments: "Here and in verse 14 the woman appears to be understood as a personification of the Christian community, which began to experience persecution following the birth and ascension of the Messiah" (Aune, Rev. Vol. 52B, p. 691). The 1260 days imply a limited time but one in which there is suffering and persecution. This symbolic number is taken from Daniel. We always are to keep in mind the victory of the Messiah (Jesus Christ) despite the hour of darkness that the prince of this world (Satan) has. In John's Gospel the same drama is described: "Now is the judgment of this world; now the ruler of this world will be driven out" (Jn 12:31).

The birth of the Messiah from this woman is part of the seer's narrative. In contemporary exegesis, most scholars give this an ecclesiological interpretation. In fact, from the time of the Apocalypse, the ecclesiological interpretation prevailed. Oecumenius (6th century), wrote that the woman is Mary who though being in the heavens is one with humanity. Saint Bonaventure (1221-1274 C.E.) says the *literal* meaning of the text pertains to Mary: the *mystical*, to the Church. Perhaps, a helpful remark of John J. Scullion, S.J. may shed some light on this somewhat ambivalent and multivalent pericope: "The Mariological meaning is part of the whole meaning which is ecclesiological. Mary is not merely a symbol of the people of God — she belongs to it. Hence, the woman is the people of God; but in the birth in v. 5 — note, the birth is a concrete event, not an abstraction — it is Mary, and with her all others as members of the community and in their various relations to this event." (*Revelation,* in *A New Catholic Commentary on Scripture,* Nelson, rev. 1975, p. 1277).

The Flashback of Rv 12:7-12: Michael Against the Dragon

This tremendous angelic conflict provides an unexpected interruption in the flow of the narrative. It is like a significant flashback in a story or movie that gives the reader an insight into the realm of the cosmic mythical battle of the good angels represented by Michael and the bad ones under the leadership of the dragon, Satan. In Luke's Gospel, Jesus himself has a similar moment of recall. The entire pericope is insightful: "The seventy returned with joy, saying, 'Lord, in your name even the demons submit to us!' He said to them, 'I watched Satan fall from heaven like a flash of lightning. See, I have given you authority to tread on snakes and scorpions, and over all the power of the enemy; and nothing will hurt you. Nevertheless, do not rejoice at this, that the spirits submit to you, but rejoice that your names are written in heaven'" (Lk 10:17-20).

In the Hebrew Scriptures Michael is the guardian angel of Israel. Michael appears only in three texts of Daniel (Dn 10:13-21; 12:1) and only in Jude 9 besides our text in the New Testament. The fact of the passive voice being used for the "cast down" of Satan indicates that God is the victor in this combat myth.

This part of the story tells how the dragon was cast down to earth thus pursuing and persecuting the woman who represents the faithful people of God, the Church. The dragon is given a list of names — his aliases, if you will. He is the Devil, Satan, and the Deceiver of the whole world. Verse 9 is the only explicit reference to Satan's being related to the serpent in Genesis 3:1-7. (See also Gn 3:15; Lk 10:19; Rm 16:20; 2 Cor 11:3, 14).

Another insight into the combat myth of Michael against the dragon is gained by looking at an ancient expulsion myth in Judaism found in Isaiah 14:12-16:

How you are fallen from heaven,
O Day Star, son of Dawn!
How you are cut down to the ground,
you who laid the nations low!
You said in your heart, "I will ascend to heaven:
I will raise my throne
above the stars of God;
I will sit on the mount of assembly
on the heights of Zaphon:
I will ascend to the tops of the clouds,
I will make myself like the Most High."
But you are brought down to Sheol,
to the depths of the Pit.
Those who see you will stare at you.

The seer gives us a moment of rest and contemplation in verses 10-12. A proclamation is heard in heaven declaring that God's Messiah (Jesus) has conquered the Accuser (Satan means adversary, accuser) of the faithful by means of the blood of the Lamb (the death of the Messiah at Passover). The witnesses in heaven are rejoicing but on earth the battle continues "for the devil has come down to you with great wrath, because he knows that his time is short" (Rv 12:12).

Michael, one of the seven archangels, means "who is like unto God?". He has in the Qumran literature affinities to Melchizedek and, of course, to Israel as its patron and defender. Some commentators have also identified Michael with Jesus, the Messiah, but this is reading more into the text than is warranted. Michael's victory is followed by the hymn of praise proclaimed in heaven. The victory has been won by the blood of Christ; salvation is assured to those who believe in and worship God and the Lamb. This contemplative moment has prepared us for the onslaught of the dragon against the woman. We turn now to the final scene of the great positive sign of the woman.

The Dragon Pursues the Woman and Her Offspring (Rv 12:13-17)

The dragon now attempts to destroy the woman. Her child, the Messiah, has been wafted to heaven (Rv 12:5). It is the rest of her offspring here on earth who are in danger of being devoured by the wrath-filled dragon. The woman is lifted to the desert by two gigantic wings of an eagle. The symbolism reminds us of Israel's flight from Pharaoh into the desert. The two wings could symbolize the *Torah* and the *Nebiim* (the Prophets) which show God's covenantal love and promises of protection for God's elect. The tribulation will not last forever. We are back to Daniel's schema for measuring time. The time, times, and a half time are the same as the 42 months and the 1260 days.

The narrator now describes the devil as the great serpent, the writhing serpent or Leviathan — probably taken from a Mesopotamian myth. In Is 27:1 we have an example of such a myth: "On that day the Lord with his cruel and great and strong sword will punish *Leviathan*, the fleeing *serpent*, Leviathan the twisting serpent, and he will kill the *dragon* that is in the sea."

Father Ignace de la Potterie, S.J., shares an experience of this scene: "In the sea aquarium of Monaco there is an enormous serpent. It is menacing and terrible to see. The twisting of his very long body disappears and reappears continually between the rocks, and the treacherous reflection of its cunning eyes gives a feeling of anguish. This monster has made me think of the dragon of Revelation 12" (*Mary in the Mystery of the Covenant*, Alba House, New York, 1992, p. 256, f.n. 25).

The waters spewing from the dragon's mouth are indicative of an attempt to destroy the woman. Torrential waters, the sea, are often threats to the person who struggles against such power in nature. Frequently, the trials expressed in the psalmist's prayers are metaphorically compared to the overwhelming waves of the sea.

Fortunately, God's protective forces in the good earth come

to her rescue and swallow up the flood-like waters issuing from the mouth of the dragon. Amidst all of the violence that appears in Revelation, these are also scenes in which the goodness of all of God's creation appear. The renewal of the earth, its protective characteristics, and its harmony with God's human creatures is symbolized in verse 16.

The final verse of chapter 12 resumes the theme of conflict between Satan and the offspring (the seed) of the woman. Genesis 3:15 is the source behind this verse. We have already seen a messianic interpretation of it in the Genesis Apocryphon.

Father de la Potterie sums up the meaning of this verse by showing us both a Marian and an ecclesial interpretation:

> The figure of the Woman in Revelation 12 has, then, a significance both ecclesial and Marian, but especially under the aspect of the maternity of the Woman in relation to her children. She is the mother of the male child which she has brought into the world but, at the spiritual level, she is also — and this holds both for Mary and the Church — mother of other children, "the rest of her descendants."

Here we need to address another detail of verse 17, which is revealing since it concerns these children of the Woman, "… notably those who *obey* God's orders and who *witness faithfully* to Jesus."

These other children are, then, the believers who, through their trials and persecution, observe the commandments of God and continue to bear witness to Jesus. Now according to the final words of Mary in the New Testament does she not say: "Do whatever He tells you" (Jn 2:5)?

As we have said in our interpretation of the messianic wedding at Cana, it concerns obedience to Jesus, of fidelity to the covenant concluded between God and his people, of openness and availability with regard to the saving initiative of God: in brief, of the profound faith, which is the door of access to the condition of spiritual childhood and which is its fundamental characteristic. This agrees with the teaching of the verse of Revelation 12:17.

Food for the Journey:
Isaiah 61:10-11

[10]I will greatly rejoice in the Lord, my whole being shall exult in my God; for he has clothed me with the garments of salvation, he has covered me with the robe of righteousness, as a bridegroom decks himself with a garland, and as a bride adorns herself with her jewels. [11]For as the earth brings forth its shoots, and as a garden causes what is sown in it to spring up, so the Lord God will cause righteousness and praise to spring up before all the nations.

Revelation 13:1-18

[1]And I saw a beast rising out of the sea, having ten horns and seven heads; and on its horns were ten diadems, and on its heads were blasphemous names. [2]And the beast that I saw was like a leopard, its feet were like a bear's, and its mouth was like a lion's mouth. And the dragon gave it his power and his throne and great authority. [3]One of its heads seemed to have received a death-blow, but its mortal wound had been healed. In amazement the whole earth followed the beast. [4]They worshiped the dragon, for he had given his authority to the beast, and they worshiped the beast, saying, "Who is like the beast, and who can fight against it?"

[5]The beast was given a mouth uttering haughty and blasphemous words, and it was allowed to exercise authority for forty-two months. [6]It opened its mouth to utter blasphemies against God, blaspheming his name and his dwelling, that is, those who dwell in heaven. [7]Also it was allowed to make war on the saints and to conquer them. It was given authority over every tribe and people and language and nation, [8]and all the inhabitants of the earth will worship it, everyone whose name has not been written from the foundation of the world in the Book of Life of the Lamb that was slaughtered.

[9]Let anyone who has an ear listen:
[10]If you are to be taken captive,
into captivity you go;

if you kill with the sword,
with the sword you must be killed.
Here is a call for the endurance and faith of the saints.

[11]Then I saw another beast that rose out of the earth; it had two horns like a lamb and it spoke like a dragon. [12]It exercises all the authority of the first beast on its behalf, and it makes the earth and its inhabitants worship the first beast, whose mortal wound had been healed. [13]It performs great signs, even making fire come down from heaven to earth in the sight of all; [14]and by the signs that it is allowed to perform on behalf of the beast, it deceives the inhabitants of earth, telling them to make an image for the beast that had been wounded by the sword and yet lived; [15]and it was allowed to give breath to the image of the beast so that the image of the beast could even speak and cause those who would not worship the image of the beast to be killed. [16]Also it causes all, both small and great, both rich and poor, both free and slave, to be marked on the right hand or the forehead, [17]so that no one can buy or sell who does not have the mark, that is, the name of the beast or the number of its name. [18]This calls for wisdom: let anyone with understanding calculate the number of the beast, for it is the number of a person. Its number is six hundred sixty-six.

John of Patmos speaks:

I shall not tarry in relation to the next sequence of my vision, for what I am now saying will make it clear that evil does not prevail. In your more modern idiom, you might say "The good guys always win in the end," but "it is not over till it is over."

In your own reading of the final redaction of the text of Revelation, chapters 13-18 are focused on the corruption and evil of the Roman Empire. The governor in Asia Minor banished me to this dreadful island called Patmos. The only good thing about this exile is my ability to remember the sacred Scriptures of my people, the Jews. You already know that I am a Christian Jew called to voice what I have experienced in an ecstatic vision.

This part of the vision is the most violent. Some of your modern critics have been so appalled by this section that they reject the narrative and criticize my patriarchal and macho approach. That may be true, but it was the only way I could express and describe the visions and share them with you. Evil is violent and obscene. My limited knowledge of Greek and my own limited first-century culture formed me into the person that I am. I am speaking the truth in what I say, but I know the imagery and metaphors and language turn many of you away from reading this revelation. You thereby deny yourself the bigger picture I was describing. You do not seem to be able to walk in my sandals and see and feel what I felt. For this reason, I have tried to simplify what I experienced. I do not mean to be offensive or manipulative with what I have written. I realize that my concept of women and my relationship to them is very limited, very awkward, and depicted in stark contrasts of black and white categories. I apologize for my cultural and religious limitation. I do ask you, however, to focus on my message of how evil eventually is overcome. Perhaps, these remarks will help you to read further and then to go back to the finished text of Revelation.

After the beautiful vision of the woman representing the churches, I saw how she was pursued by the dragon. This is where we are in my mystical experience. All that follows is a series of scenes that show the powerful forces of the dragon. They are represented by two beasts, one of whom is the emperor who has come back to life as Nero (*redivivus*) and a second beast which is the personification of the empire. The legendary image of Nero (the 666 of the code which is the numerical equivalent of NRON KSR), says that he would unite himself with the Parthians at the Euphrates River and conquer those parts of the empire that were lost. The Romans of my time only feared one people — the Parthians.

God is merciful even in a mystical experience. I now see the Lamb standing on Mount Zion. It is he who will overcome the devil (dragon) and the beasts. God's angel cries out: "Fear God and give him glory for the hour of his judgment has come. Worship him who made heaven and earth, the sea and the springs of water." Another angel shouts: "Fallen, fallen is Babylon the great who has made the nations drink the wine of her fornication." I realized how the holy ones who were martyred no longer suffered; I also realized God's harvest was taking place and the evil and the good would be separated through the angel's sickle.

I will give you a clue: the seven seals, trumpets, and now the seven bowls filled with the plagues are a recapitulation of what is central to my experience. God will overcome evil in myriad ways through the judgment to be given to the beasts, the followers of Satan, and to the harlot who represents Rome. These last seven bowls of God's wrath are experienced by the inhabitants of the earth just as Pharaoh and his people experienced the plagues in Egypt. The plagues are uninterrupted and are similar to several of those during the Exodus from Egypt.

I am now dumbstruck for a sensuous woman dressed in purple and scarlet suddenly appears before me. There is something alluring and attractive about her. She is decked out with pearls and gold chains. She undoubtedly is the exact opposite of the first woman I saw. I realized her symbolic meaning. The harlot is the political-religious and economic power of the luxurious Roman Empire. She stands out against the sky, mounted on a beast, offering her pleasures to kings, merchants, and seafarers. She hates the woman clothed in white who symbolizes the churches and those who are faithful to God's commandments. The whore only recognizes those signed with the mark of the beast on their forehead and right hand. The woman, the harlot, is the great city that holds sway over the kings of the earth.

I heard her name "Babylon." This is not good news for my Jewish ears; nor for me as a Christian inasmuch as I recognized it as the code name of Roma, the goddess of the empire, and its capital city. She was drunk with the blood of the martyrs. She was obscene, haughty, and insolent. I marveled at her sensuous beauty. Fortunately, the angel reminded me who she really is and where I am in all of this. Babylon would soon be coming to an end. A dirge was then chanted by her admirers: "Woe, woe, the great metropolis, mighty woman Babylon! In one hour your doom has come!" The dirge started with the rulers; the merchants took up its refrain; finally, the robust seafarers wailed out the same words: "Babylon! woe, woe, woe, great city that you were, you are now fallen, fallen, fallen!"

Then almost like the victory shouts at a colosseum I heard the holy ones chanting "Hallelujah! The smoke from her goes up forever! Amen! Hallelujah!" I sensed that evil was at its end and I was soon to experience something great, something good. I could hardly wait to see and hear what was to follow.

COMMENTARY

Revelation 13:1-18

This entire chapter focuses on the forces of evil unleashed through the two beasts. Both get their power (*exousia*) from the dragon who is their master. The antagonists are fully described in order that the great conflict between the powers of heaven and those of hell or the underworld are lined up in battle. Repetition of key words dramatizes the colossal feats of the beasts to show how overwhelming the struggle will be for God's faithful people living on the earth.

Actually this section may start with the last phrase of chapter 12, verse 18, where the manuscripts have the following variants: one reading would be "He, that is, the dragon, stood on the sand of the sea." This would end chapter twelve with a concluding mention of the dragon. The second reading would refer to John of Patmos standing on the sand or beach and then describe what he sees. Thus 12:18 could introduce this new visual experience of the visionary. Aune in his meticulous exegetical work on Revelation favors the inclusion of verse 18 with the dragon standing on the sand of the sea and has the expression "Then I (John) saw..." as the introduction to a vision formula (Aune, Vol. 52B, p. 722).

Aune's arguments are cogent from the inner world of the text, for a parallel vision formula occurs in verse 11a when John says for the second time, "Then I saw...." This formula refers to the appearance of the second beast. Aune also posits the references to the dragon in this section (12:18-13:18) as redactional or the work of the final editor of Revelation. Our unit contains two parts: first, the beast from the sea (Rv 12:18-13:10) and then the beast from the land (Rv 13:12-18).

The Beast from the Sea (Rv 12:18-13:10)

The dragon waits for the emergence of the first beast from the sea. In Jewish apocryphal works this beast can be compared to the sea monster Leviathan or Lotan. In a Ugaritic myth Leviathan battles with Baal siding with Mot, god of the underworld. The symbolism of the monster appears already in the fifth day of creation in Genesis 1. Leviathan is also mentioned in the Psalms 74:13-14; 104:26; and in Job we also find references to such a mythical beast (Job 3:8; 26:12-13; 41:1-34).

The beast is represented as having great power through the symbolism of the ten horns, and universal rule over the earth through the seven heads. The four comparative beast-like parts of this sea monster issue from Daniel 7:2-7 and can show that the extent of the Roman empire is over the whole world for it has conquered all the other beasts whether the leopard, the bear, or the lion.

Frequently, the sea monster represented the foreign powers and enemies of Israel; now the reigning authority is Rome which has imperial sway over Judaism and Christianity. Behind the wounded head is the legend about Nero who died on June 9, 68 C.E. People feared and honored his reputation so much in Asia that there was a rumor he had been restored to life — probably reincarnated in the emperor Domitian. This is the famous legend of Nero *redivivus*. In Italy, Nero was feared. He had murdered his mother and two of his wives. He also used the Christians as a scape-goat for the fires started in Rome in 64 C.E. Many were martyred probably including the apostles Peter and Paul. Nero committed suicide, but there were rumors that he would return. Finally, in the last line of this present chapter of Revelation, Nero is the leading candidate for the riddle of the person or power behind the num-ber 666. We must keep in mind that the number is symbolic and could apply to Roman authority in general. In favor of the num-ber itself is the fact that the expression NRON KSR, "Nero Cae-sar," comes closest to 666 if the Jewish system of gematria is used. Incidentally, a professor of Judaism named Eric Friedland, a dear friend, proposed this solution to me while using gematria. Again, Aune gives full treatment of the riddle (AB, pp. 770-773). Aune summarizes his treatment in this manner: "The coded name of the first beast is 666, a number that is the total of the numerical value of the letters spelling "Nero Caesar" in Aramaic (found in a docu-ment in Palestine at Wadi Muraba'at), though this is just one of the many possible solutions to the riddle" (Vol. 52B, p. 780).

In this story about the two beasts, we realize that the seer is offering us an allegorical tale which springs from the prophet Daniel on the first level of reading (see Dn 7:3-7; 8:10-14). On another level it seems to be referring to the seven Caesars from Nero (54-68 C.E.) to Domitian (81-96 C.E.).

On a third level it is the mythical combat of Leviathan the sea monster, and, in part two of Behemoth, the land monster. Fi-nally, on a fourth level it is a parody of Jesus, the Lamb. All the honor and worship given to God and the Lamb in chapter five is now contrasted with the world's worship of the dragon and the two beasts. This chaotic reversal is the antithesis of what the seven churches are summoned to do. They are always to worship God and to abhor the prayers, incense, and sacrifices offered to the Roman Emperor and his satellites in Asia. Even the refrain "Who is like the beast, and who can fight against it?" (v. 4) is a parody on the praises due to God and the Lamb.

The blasphemous names given to the beast are the reversal

of titles belonging to God and to Christ. We have already heard these laudatory descriptions and title in chapter one. Domitian had the boldness to use the expression "who was and is and is to be" as a title belonging to him as emperor.

John, the seer, may also be recalling the ruthless Antiochus Epiphanes who is described as the "little horn" in Daniel 7:23. His arrogance and desecration of the temple with his image is mirrored in John's description of the blasphemies uttered by the beast. The duration of 42 months is also taken from Daniel. Here it represents the eschatological dimension of trampling what is sacred to the seven churches and to Christianity. The lines are being drawn for the ultimate combat: good against the evil of the dragon and the beasts; chaos and darkness against the order and heavenly realm of light and true worship.

Everything is now happening on earth. This phrase "upon the earth" (*epi tes ges*) comes in rhythmic patterns. The war against the saints is about to take place here on earth. The empire has total dominion over all tribes, people, languages, and nations. The saints are about to be conquered or inveigled into this false superpower of arrogance, opulence, and blasphemy.

Verse 8 reads better if we take the translation of the New Revised Standard Version: "whose name has not been written from the foundation of the world in the Book of Life of the Lamb that was slaughtered." A parallel passage from Rv 17:8 helps us see this as the meaning intended by the narrator. In the latter passage no mention is made of the slaughtered Lamb. However, there is a passage in 1 P 1:18-20 which reads: "You know that you were ransomed from the futile ways inherited from your ancestors, not with perishable things like silver or gold, but with the precious blood of Christ, like that of a lamb without defect or blemish. He was destined *before the foundation of the world*, but was revealed at the end of the ages for your sake." The second reading of Rv 13:8 then would see the saving plan of God through Christ even before the world was created.

Verse 9 is an exhortation to listen and to understand, similar to what we have seen in the messages to the churches. A citation from Jeremiah follows (cf. Jr 15:2; 43:11). The captivity the saints must undergo or martyrdom by the sword — a favorite of the Romans! — would lead the saints to dogged endurance of their trials through faith in God and the Lamb.

The Second Beast (Rv 13:11-18)

With the second beast from the land, the allegory continues on several levels. Behemoth, the land beast, is the masculine counterpart to Leviathan, the feminine sea beast. On the historical level, the emperor Domitian is the first to demand divine honor during his lifetime. At Ephesus, a gigantic statue was erected in his likeness, and was honored. From the writer Pliny we know that Christians were forced to offer wine and water to the emperor in Bithynia in 112 C.E.

There is "magic" and "mystery" connected with such rites of emperor worship. Fire from the heavens and speaking statues were part of this cultic magic. It could well be that this second beast symbolizes the religious and priestly dimension of the empire. It is totally dependent on the first beast for its power and authority, but at the local shrines it exudes its own magic.

Both soldiers and slaves were marked with signs of the emperor and his beloved Rome. We notice attention placed on the hands — they are marked with signs enabling them to buy and sell. The forehead is also marked with a sign, in contrast to those righteous who have been marked with the sign of a Christian. Could this refer to the cross and to baptism? Perhaps, for the Roman citizens both in Italy and in the outlying districts of Asia, the tattooing of the name of a god or the emperor is what is meant by the narrator.

We must remain sane when looking at the riddle offered at the end of chapter 13. Unfortunately, eisegesis and prejudice have influenced many a reader and commentator. The Book of Revelation is not an oracle of predictions for our time that are so specific as to name contemporaries. In the history of traditional interpretation several Popes have been so named as being 666 (Leo X comes to mind). Even recently it was heard that it would match Ronald Reagan if his middle initial or name is used. Symbolism is not to be given over to mathematical or prejudicial precision. The number 666 shows incompleteness: deception, falsity. As mentioned above, by taking the Aramaic inscription found in Wadi Murraba'at we can use gematria for deciphering *NRON KSR* (Nero Caesar) which results in 666. The fact that we are within the measure of time appropriate for the Apocalypse makes Nero a leading candidate; but, remember, this is a symbolic number.

Food for the Journey:

2 Thessalonians 2:3-11

> [3]Let no one deceive you in any way; for that day will not come unless the rebellion comes first and the lawless one is revealed, the one destined for destruction. [4]He opposes and exalts himself above every so-called god or object of worship, so that he takes his seat in the temple of God, declaring himself to be God. [5]Do you not remember that I told you these things when I was still with you? [6]And you know what is now restraining him, so that he may be revealed when his time comes. [7]For the mystery of lawlessness is already at work, but only until the one who now restrains it is removed. [8]And then the lawless one will be revealed, whom the Lord Jesus will destroy with the breath of his mouth, annihilating him by the manifestation of his coming. [9]The coming of the lawless one is apparent in the working of Satan, who uses all power, signs, lying wonders, [10]and every kind of wicked deception for those who are perishing, because they refused to love the truth and so be saved. [11]For this reason God sends them a powerful delusion, leading them to believe what is false.

CHAPTER SIX

THE SEVEN FINAL PLAGUES
(Rv 14-18)

Revelation 14:1-20

[1]Then I looked, and there was the Lamb, standing on Mount Zion! And with him were one hundred forty-four thousand who had his name and his Father's name written on their foreheads. [2]And I heard a voice from heaven like the sound of many waters and like the sound of loud thunder; the voice I heard was like the sound of harpists playing on their harps, [3]and they sing a new song before the throne and before the four living creatures and before the elders. No one could learn that song except the one hundred forty-four thousand who have been redeemed from the earth. [4]It is these who have not defiled themselves with women, for they are virgins; these follow the Lamb wherever he goes. They have been redeemed from humankind as first fruits for God and the Lamb, [5]and in their mouth no lie was found; they are blameless.

[6]Then I saw another angel flying in midheaven, with an eternal gospel to proclaim to those who live on the earth — to every nation and tribe and language and people. [7]He said in a loud voice, "Fear God and give him glory, for the hour of his judgment has come; and worship him who made heaven and earth, the sea and the springs of water."

[8]Then another angel, a second, followed, saying, "Fallen, fallen is Babylon the great! She has made all nations drink of the wine of the wrath of her fornication."

[9]Then another angel, a third, followed them, crying with a loud voice, "Those who worship the beast and its image, and receive a mark on their foreheads or on their hands, [10]they will also drink the wine of God's wrath, poured unmixed into the cup of his anger, and they will be tormented with fire and sulfur in the presence of the holy angels and in the presence of the Lamb. [11]And the smoke of their torment goes up forever and ever. There is no rest day or night for those who worship the beast and its image and for anyone who receives the mark of its name."

[12]Here is a call for the endurance of the saints, those who keep the commandments of God and hold fast to the faith of Jesus.

[13]And I heard a voice from heaven saying, "Write this: Blessed are the dead who from now on die in the Lord." "Yes," says the Spirit, "they will rest from their labors, for their deeds follow them."

[14]Then I looked, and there was a white cloud, and seated on the cloud was one like the Son of Man, with a golden crown on his head, and a sharp sickle in his hand! [15]Another angel came out of the temple, calling with a loud voice to the one who sat on the cloud, "Use your sickle and reap, for the hour to reap has come, because the harvest of the earth is fully ripe." [16]So the one who sat on the cloud swung his sickle over the earth, and the earth was reaped.

[17]Then another angel came out of the temple in heaven, and he too had a sharp sickle. [18]Then another angel came out from the altar, the angel who has authority over fire, and he called with a loud voice to him who had the sharp sickle, "Use your sharp sickle and gather the clusters of the vine of the earth, for its grapes are ripe." [19]So the angel swung his sickle over the earth and gathered the vintage of the earth, and he threw it into the great wine press of the wrath of God. [20]And the wine press was trodden outside the city, and blood flowed from the wine press, as high as a horse's bridle, for a distance of about two hundred miles.

COMMENTARY

A Glimpse into the Final Time: Salvation and Judgment (Rv 14:1-20)

If one reads the manuscripts carefully, seven angels are implied. However, in a literal counting of this vision only six are mentioned. The implied reading of seven angels is the more difficult (*lectio difficilior*) and, therefore, is considered by exegetes to be the original text. But symbolic literature and apocalyptic descriptions are not logical or always orderly. Moreover, we are in the midst of a breathtaking vision of the earthly and heavenly voyager, John of Patmos. Personally, this author thinks this consoling scene is characteristic of the visionary's patterns of thought flowing from an ecstatic experience. Once again we are given a moment of contemplative wonder at what it will be like as salvation and judgment meet. The welcomed pause is necessary, for the most violent scenes of the war scroll are to be followed with the outpouring of the seven bowls of wrath (Rv 15:1-16:21) and the total destruction of the whore called Babylon (the Roman Empire and culture). Chapter 17 will show the woman in scarlet condemned, and her total collapse will be seen in chapter 18.

The Lamb and the Virgins (Rv 14:1-5)

The words of the seer are put into a prophetic formula which describes his vision: "I saw... and behold the Lamb!" In another writing of the Johannine school a similar prophecy was made by another prophet John who declared, "The next day John saw Jesus coming to him, and he said, 'Behold, the lamb of God, who takes away the sin of the world!'" (Jn 1:36). The Lamb is the Messiah Jesus who as a Davidid, victoriously stands on Mount Zion, which is the original site of David's city of Jerusalem.

The 144,000 of a special portion of the elect have already been described in chapter 7. The background of the Exodus and the destruction of the Egyptian charioteers is helpful for understanding the meaning of those named as virgins. During the "sacred war" abstention from sexual love was a cultic as well as military requirement. It is vain reasoning to associate this unusual statement with our contemporary insights into the notion of virginity and celibacy. This has nothing to do with, or to say about, religious vows of poverty, chastity, and obedience. In the Apocalypse we are immersed in the sacred war of God's elect against the forces of Satan symbolized by the Roman Empire.

The signing of the 144,000 recalls the Passover symbol of being signed with the blood of the lamb now transformed into being signed with the name of God presented as the Father. These people are also unblemished like the Paschal Lamb whom they follow. The scene is profoundly descriptive since a new song is being sung (recall the Song of Moses and/or Miriam in Exodus 15). Only those in the heavenly court could sing this song of victory with the accompanying harpists and they sounded like the modern boom boxes and the waterfalls of Niagara. The witness of the elect is bound up with truth and integrity; lies, deception, and trickery belong to Satan and his cohorts.

The Proclamations of Three Angels (Rv 14:6-11)

The first angel has the positive side of an eternal message for the faithful. This good news is intended for everyone upon the earth — all tribes, nations, peoples, and languages. They are called to witness the God of all creation (Gn 1:1-2:4a is cultic and is attributed to the Priestly Tradition). The response of the faithful is to "fear God and give him honor" (v. 7). This is the same as the overall and final message of Revelation: "Worship God."

The second angel proclaims negatively that Babylon (Rome) has fallen because of her wrath and immorality.

The third angel of this passage warns that those who accept the sign of the beast upon their forehead and their hand will experience the wrath of God's judgment while the Lamb and the angels look on. The torment is described in terms similar to the fall of Sodom and Gomorrah (Gn 19:23-29). The judgment of God falls upon those who worship the beast by receiving the mark of his name. Judgment and salvation are contrasted in this scene of the three angels; the free choice of each person decides which angelic message will be received.

The Blessedness of the Saints (Rv 14:12-13)

This is one of the most beautiful messages in the Book of Revelation. The selection is aptly used in the rite of Christian burial as one of the possible readings. The good works of a person accompany her or him into the realm of heaven. The patient endurance of God's pilgrim people is rewarded for they have kept the commandments of God and witnessed to Jesus the Lamb. The seer then hears another beatitude (there are seven beatitudes in the Apocalypse): "Blessed are the dead who die in the Lord." We may think of the passage of Jesus telling us, "Learn from me for I am meek and humble of heart, and you will find rest for your souls. For my yoke is easy, and my burden light" (Mt 11:29-30).

Vision of the Angelic Reapers of the Earth (Rv 14:14-20)

Most commentators see the expression "one like the son of man" (one like a human being) as referring to Jesus as the Christ. It is possible that the same expression could be interpreted as another angel. Daniel 7:13 is the source for this phrase both in Rv 1:13 and in our present verse 14. In the Gospels of Matthew and Mark the angels are seen as the reapers of the harvest (Mt 13:39; Mk 13:26-27). It is the son of man who sends these angels to harvest the earth.

The first angel harvests the grain. This harvest is clearly a metaphor for the eschatological judgment of God upon human-kind. It is possible that the first harvest is intended for the nations while the harvest of the vineyard pertains to the chosen of God, Israel.

The image of the son of man wearing a golden wreath symbolizes authority and victory. The 24 elders are also wearing gold wreaths (Rv 4:4,10). The sharp sickle is a sign that the grapes are ready for harvesting.

Aune thinks that the second angel who commands the first indicates that the expression "son of man" would mean an angelic creature not the Lamb or Jesus as Messiah. This is a good insight, but we have to remember that symbolic language is not always logical, and theological insights often influence one's interpretation.

The fact that the narrative mentions the "hour" of harvest again helps us see an important eschatological moment. This is it! There is both a positive dimension to the harvest and a negative one. The first angel swings a sharp sickle to harvest the grain. However, the second and third angels are using their sickles to harvest the grapes — and it is through this harvest that the negative features of ultimate judgment and decision are brought out.

The prophet Joel is a most likely source for this section of the vision about the harvesting of the vineyard on earth. The third chapter of Joel offers us a similar metaphor for God's judgment of the nations. Here is a citation that uses an image like that from the book of Revelation: "The nations must get ready and come to the Valley of Judgment. There I, the Lord, will sit to judge all the surrounding nations. They are very wicked; cut them down like grain at harvest time; crush them as grapes are crushed in a full winepress until the wine runs over." ... "The Lord roars from Mount Zion; his voice thunders from Jerusalem; earth and sky tremble. But he will defend his people" (Jl 3:12-13,16).

The reference to the great winepress of the wrath of God outside the city may refer to the great amount of blood to be shed in the final eschatological battle. Just as Jesus poured out his blood on Calvary outside the city of Jerusalem, so, too, will the divine wrath of God's judgment bring about the blood shedding of those guilty of killing so many witnesses, both in the first and the second covenants. In the final battle the blood of the Lamb will be victorious over death, evil, and sin. The symbolic number of 1600 stadia is taken to mean the whole earth. There was an old Jewish tradition that the Last Judgment will take place in the valley of Jehoshaphat outside the city of Jerusalem.

There seems to be a connection between the mention of the bridles of the horses with a heavenly army who fight against the persecutors and followers of the beast. In the nineteenth chapter, Christ is the victorious leader who rides a white horse; his robe has been dipped in blood. He is the Word of God. On his thigh is inscribed the name, "King of kings and Lord of lords" (Rv 19:11-16).

Food for the Journey:

Isaiah 40:9-11

> [9]Get you up to a high mountain, O Zion, herald of good tidings; lift up your voice with strength, O Jerusalem, herald of good tidings, lift it up, do not fear; say to the cities of Judah, "Here is your God!" [10]See, the Lord God comes with might, and his arm rules for him; his reward is with him, and his recompense before him. [11]He will feed his flock like a shepherd; he will gather the lambs in his arms, and carry them in his bosom, and gently lead the mother sheep.

Revelation 15:1-8

> [1]Then I saw another portent in heaven, great and amazing: seven angels with seven plagues, which are the last, for with them the wrath of God is ended. [2]And I saw what appeared to be a sea of glass mixed with fire, and those who had conquered the beast and its image and the number of its name, standing beside the sea of

glass with harps of God in their hands. ³And they sing the song of Moses, the servant of God, and the song of the Lamb: "Great and amazing are your deeds, Lord God the Almighty! Just and true are your ways, King of the nations! ⁴Lord, who will not fear and glorify your name? For you alone are holy. All nations will come and worship before you, for your judgments have been revealed." ⁵After this I looked, and the temple of the tent of witness in heaven was opened, ⁶and out of the temple came the seven angels with the seven plagues, robed in pure bright linen, with golden sashes across their chests. ⁷Then one of the four living creatures gave the seven angels seven golden bowls full of the wrath of God, who lives forever and ever; ⁸and the temple was filled with smoke from the glory of God and from his power, and no one could enter the temple until the seven plagues of the seven angels were ended.

The Seven Last Plagues (Rv 15:1-8)

This is the shortest chapter in the Apocalypse. It's imagery is dependent on the plagues inflicted upon Pharaoh in the Book of Exodus, chapters 13-15. The unit focuses on the seven angels who will be given seven bowls containing the seven last plagues of God's wrath to be poured out upon the earth and on those in league with the beast.

The first part of the vision takes place in heaven where a third and last great sign is given. This sign consists of the seven angels with the seven bowls filled with the seven last plagues. Remember that the last two signs are negative in the effect they have upon the earth; the first sign, that of the woman clothed with the sun is positive and filled with hope because of God's protection.

The Triumph of the Faithful (Rv 15:1-4)

Just as the seventh seal was prefaced by a transition before it was broken, so, too, in this vision the seer has a vision of the faithful before God. They are singing a new song like that of Moses. Theirs is a New Exodus which has brought them to the promised realm of God. Their song is majestic and triumphant. It is a hymn which captures the ethos of the entire Apocalypse. God alone is being glorified and honored. This adoration of the Almighty is continued forever in the heavens. God alone is central to every being that surrounds the celestial throne. This is the seventh vision in the present cycle and the theme of salvation is emphasized next to that of adoration. The transition in the unnumbered cycle of the central part of Revelation leads to the seven vials filled with the plagues, the signs of God's wrath (Rv 12:1-15:4).

The triumphant faithful have not worshiped the beast, nor his mark, nor the enigmatic and sinister number of the beast. Again, such a contemplative pause is necessary for the story as we approach the seven plagues.

We also notice that God's universal justice is being celebrated through the salvation of those who were witnesses to God and to the Lamb. This celebration is in contrast to the former vision of the 144,000 which was more a celebration of individual salvation.

This transitional scene is also connected with chapter fourteen in the vision of the grain harvest and the vineyard wherein God's just judgement is displayed through three angels (Rv 14:6-13; 14:14-20).

Food for the Journey:

Wisdom of Solomon 18:13-19

[13]For though they had disbelieved everything because of their magic arts, yet, when their firstborn were destroyed, they acknowledged your people to be God's child. [14]For while gentle silence enveloped all things, and night in its swift course was now half

gone, [15]your all powerful word leaped from heaven, from the royal throne, into the midst of the land that was doomed, a stern warrior [16]carrying the sharp sword of your authentic command, and stood and filled all things with death, and touched heaven while standing on the earth. [17]Then at once apparitions in dreadful dreams greatly troubled them, and unexpected fears assailed them; [18]and one here and another there, hurled down half dead, made known why they were dying; [19]for the dreams that disturbed them forewarned them of this, so that they might not perish without knowing why they suffered.

Revelation 16:1-21

[1]Then I heard a loud voice from the temple telling the seven angels, "Go and pour out on the earth the seven bowls of the wrath of God." [2]So the first angel went and poured his bowl on the earth, and a foul and painful sore came on those who had the mark of the beast and who worshiped its image. [3]The second angel poured his bowl into the sea, and it became like the blood of a corpse, and every living thing in the sea died. [4]The third angel poured his bowl into the rivers and the springs of water, and they became blood. [5]And I heard the angel of the waters say, "You are just, O Holy One, who are and were, for you have judged these things; [6]because they shed the blood of saints and prophets, you have given them blood to drink. It is what they deserve!" [7]And I heard the altar respond, "Yes, O Lord God, the Almighty, your judgments are true and just!" [8]The fourth angel poured his bowl on the sun, and it was allowed to scorch people with fire; [9]they were scorched by the fierce heat, but they cursed the name of God, who had authority over these plagues, and they did not repent and give him glory. [10]The fifth angel poured his bowl on the throne of the beast, and its kingdom was plunged into darkness; people gnawed their tongues in agony, [11]and cursed the God of heaven because of their pains and sores, and they did not repent of their deeds. [12]The sixth angel poured his bowl on the great river Euphrates, and its water was dried up in order to prepare the way for the kings

from the east. [13]And I saw three foul spirits like frogs coming from the mouth of the dragon, from the mouth of the beast, and from the mouth of the false prophet. [14]These are demonic spirits, performing signs, who go abroad to the kings of the whole world, to assemble them for battle on the great day of God the Almighty. [15]("See, I am coming like a thief! Blessed is the one who stays awake and is clothed, not going about naked and exposed to shame.") [16]And they assembled them at the place that in Hebrew is called Harmagedon. [17]The seventh angel poured his bowl into the air, and a loud voice came out of the temple, from the throne, saying, "It is done!" [18]And there came flashes of lightning, rumblings, peals of thunder, and a violent earthquake, such as had not occurred since people were upon the earth, so violent was that earthquake. [19]The great city was split into three parts, and the cities of the nations fell. God remembered great Babylon and gave her the wine-cup of the fury of his wrath. [20]And every island fled away, and no mountains were to be found; [21]and huge hailstones, each weighing about a hundred pounds, dropped from heaven on people, until they cursed God for the plague of the hail, so fearful was that plague.

The Wrath of God: The Seven Bowls (Rv 16:1-21)

The seven plagues, which follow in an uninterrupted sequence, are the last of the plagues mentioned in Revelation. The first two series of plagues were interrupted between the sixth and the seventh seals and trumpets.

The seven plagues poured out from the seven bowls have a resemblance to some of the plagues narrated in the Book of Exodus 7:20-10:21. The similarities are seen in the following chart:

First bowl plague   = sixth plague of Exodus 9:8-12
Second bowl plague = first plague of Exodus 7:14-15
Third bowl plague   = also Exodus 7:20-21 (first plague)
Fourth bowl plague = seventh plague of Exodus 9:22-24
Fifth bowl plague   = ninth plague of Exodus 10:21

Sixth bowl plague has no explicit plague in Exodus.

The seventh bowl plague refers to the destruction of Rome symbolized under the name Babylon. There is no counterpart in the book of Exodus.

These final plagues are parallel to those already seen in the seven seals series and in the blaring of the seven trumpets. The narrative, however, clearly reminds the reader of the Exodus event and the final description pertains to the whole world at the end time. These bowls filled with the wrath of God are spelled out through plagues which affect humans, all other forms of life, and nature itself. The narrative, filled with heavy description, is leading to the destructive climactic scene of the scarlet harlot, Babylon, who personifies Rome and all of its worldly power, allurement, and riches.

Adele Yarbro Collins describes this last series for us: "Much of the cycle of the seven bowls is an elaboration of what was already announced in the message of the second angel — 'Fallen, fallen is Babylon the great, she who made all nations drink the wine of her impure passion' (14:8). The purpose of this cycle is to portray God's justice in a symbolic way" (*The Apocalypse*, NTM 22, p. 108).

Our scene starts in the heavenly court where the archetype of the temple in Jerusalem exists. A loud voice now summons seven angels to pour out God's wrath through bowls filled with plagues. The earthly temple cult shows the priests carrying out bronze basins filled with the ashes and remains of the sacrifices: "You shall make pots for it to receive its ashes, and shovels and basins and forks and firepans; you shall make all of its utensils of bronze" (Ex 27:3).

God's wrath is contained in these bowls. Here the symbolism is imaged and understood through a passage from Jr 25:15-16: "For thus the Lord, the God of Israel, said to me: 'Take from my hand this cup of the wine of wrath, and make all the nations to whom I send you drink it. They shall drink and stagger and go out of their minds because of the sword I am sending among them.'" This drinking from the cup of wrath is symbolic of divine punishment. It is interesting that this same passage envisions destruction of the enemies of Israel including Babylon. The captivity of Babylon is to be ended once the plagues of God's wrath are poured out.

The first angel spills out the first plague which directly affects those who have worshiped the beast and its image. They are infected with foul and painful sores which are God's affliction on them for bearing the mark of the beast. These are the followers of Rome who have kowtowed to its policies and religion. A similarity to the sixth plague of Exodus is apparent: "So they took soot from the kiln, and stood before Pharaoh, and Moses threw it in the air, and it caused festering boils on humans and animals" (Ex 9:10).

The second angel empties the bowl upon the sea and all living creatures in the sea perish. The prophetic voice of God declares to Moses: "Thus says the Lord, 'By this you shall know that I am the Lord.' See, with the staff that is in my hand I will strike the water that is in the Nile, and it shall be turned into blood. The fish in the river shall die, the river itself shall stink, and the Egyptians shall be unable to drink water from the Nile" (Ex 7:17-18).

The third angel poisons the rivers and fountains of water just as the second had poisoned the sea. The first plague in Exodus is the archetype for the second and third plagues in Revelation.

This third angel is called the angel of the waters. This angel has to announce the justice and holiness of God and give the reason for the plagues. The visionary, John of Patmos, frequently experiences such a heavenly moment of God's presence whenever something dreadful and devastating occurs. The awful power of the first three plagues calls forth such a proclamation. God who is ever present in these final plagues is holy and just. God is punishing those who have shed the blood of the prophets and the martyrs. The followers of the beast are now to experience what they have unjustly meted out to God's faithful witnesses. "It is what they deserve!" (Rv 16:6).

The voice of the altar (for so reads the text) confirms the declaration of the angel of the waters: "Yes, O Lord God, the Almighty, your judgments are true and just."

Now the fourth angel pours the bowl of God's wrath over the sun. The offenders of God's holiness and justice are scorched by its fierce heat. Like their leader, Satan, and the beast, these enemies of the prophets and saints curse God and refuse, like Pharaoh, to repent. This theme of non-repentance is characteristic of the plague tradition (Ex 7:13; 22:8-15).

The fifth bowl is poured out over the throne of the beast (Rome); his kingdom is darkened and the people of the beast curse God while gnawing their tongues in agony. Again a dramatic refrain is heard: "and they did not repent of their deeds." The ninth plague of Exodus is similar to this fifth bowl with its plague. Thick darkness invaded Egypt for a period of three days (Ex 10:21-29; Ws 17:1-18:4). This darkness will be characteristic of the final days of judgment in apocalyptic accounts.

Our visionary is not only experiencing such a vision; he is also realizing that his own Hebrew Scriptures have filled his mind and memory with the events of past salvation history. God is ever present in the renewal of the prophetic promises and historic interventions of the salvation of Israel. The fidelity and continuity of God are now put forth for the followers of the Lamb and the true worshipers of the God "who was and who is" (Rv 16:5a).

Revelation 16:12-16

Rumors can be frightening; Nero was a terrifying ruler of Rome who persecuted and killed many Jews and Christians. A rumor that is behind some of the lines of Revelation claimed Nero had returned to life despite the fact of his dreadful demise. He would in his new life lead the Parthians whose boundaries were the Tigris and Euphrates Rivers to conquer the entire empire. Parthians were excellent warriors who pursued enemies with their crossbow. The speed of their cavalry was well known. Thus when the sixth angel dried up the waters of the Euphrates it was a sign that the Parthians were free to cross over and vanquish the Romans in their eastern provinces. Resurrected, too, are the dragon, the beast, and the false prophet. They are filthy with evil power and immorality. The frogs which issue from their mouths symbolize this filth and evil.

In this entire passage there continues the ironic reversal of Exodus. These beasts and unclean creatures reflect the magical powers of the Egyptian sorcerers. They are demonstrating untold powers that would inveigh even against God. In choosing the symbolism of the unclean and ugly creature the frog, we come to realize how revolting an image it is. Seán P. Kealy offers a rich description: "For the Persians the frog was the double of Ahriman, the god of evil and the agent of plagues. For the Egyptians the frog was a symbol of Hegt the goddess of fertility and resurrection. But such symbolism was a form of idolatry for the Jewish people and an indication of demonic influence (Rv 9:20; 1 Cor 10:20f.). Slimy and ugly with their useless and ceaseless croaking, frogs provided a devastating caricature of the evil monsters which the early Christian feared, the demonic influence of the state and its fawning sycophants" (*The Apocalypse of John*, Glazier, Wilmington, Delaware, 1987, p. 197).

The battle lines are set against each other on the great day of the Lord. But before the site of the gruesome conflict is mentioned, the narrator supplies us with an aside which both warns and commends. The words are those of Jesus comforting the faithful witnesses: "See I am coming like a thief! Blessed is the one who stays awake and is clothed, not going about naked and exposed to shame" (Rv 16:15).

Armageddon is the site of many of the great battles in ancient times (see Jg 5:19; 2 K 23:29-30). The words are "a Greek transliteration for the Mount of Megiddo — a famous pass through the plain of Esdraelon in Israel where armies from the North and South often clashed" (Brown, *Introduction*, p. 793, f.n. 42). Again we are led to the conclusion that no precise moment in history is meant by this final battle. The name itself is symbolic and only God knows the precise time for this ultimate act. The faithful have nothing to fear for the victory over evil has been accomplished through the Lamb's being slaughtered outside the city of Jerusalem. His blood has cleansed us of all evil, sin, and death. Armageddon is a symbol that calls for our watchfulness and attentiveness to the presence of God in the midst of world chaos.

The seventh plague is climactic and will transit into the awesome and tantalizing description of the great scarlet-clothed whore of Babylon. Like the assembly of the seven angels at the beginning of this scene, the seventh angel pours out his bowl of God's wrath into the air — almost like the horror of germ warfare! The voice from God's mystical temple declares, "It is done!" While reading these words of the last plague, one thinks of the final words of Jesus in John's Gospel, "It is finished!" (Jn 19:30).

This author believes the death of Jesus on Calvary is a key toward understanding the symbolism of many of the scenes and passages in Revelation. His victorious death is also in the present pericope which centers on the great theophany surrounding the seventh plague. All seems darkest in his life as he pours out his blood mingled with water. And yet it is in this great sacrificial moment that the Christian community is being born. Nature responds to this event with thunder, lightning and earthquakes. The prince of darkness has his hour, but the dawn of a new era breaks forth in the resurrection of the Paschal Lamb who had been slaughtered.

With chapters 17-18 we are at the denouement of the book of Revelation. First, the fall of "Babylon" is brilliantly described with a metaphor of the great harlot representing Rome and its Empire, then a cadenced dirge describing the sad feelings of it's worshipers at her demise. The victory of Christ and his Church follows with paeans of joy resounding in the heavens (19:1-10).

Food for the Journey:

Matthew 27:51-54

⁵¹At that moment the curtain of the temple was torn in two, from top to bottom. The earth shook, and the rocks were split. ⁵²The

tombs also were opened, and many bodies of the saints who had fallen asleep were raised. [53]After his resurrection they came out of the tombs and entered the holy city and appeared to many. [54]Now when the centurion and those with him, who were keeping watch over Jesus, saw the earthquake and what took place, they were terrified and said, "Truly this man was God's Son!"

Revelation 17:1-18

[1]Then one of the seven angels who had the seven bowls came and said to me, "Come, I will show you the judgment of the great whore who is seated on many waters, [2]with whom the kings of the earth have committed fornication, and with the wine of whose fornication the inhabitants of the earth have become drunk." [3]So he carried me away in the spirit into a wilderness, and I saw a woman sitting on a scarlet beast that was full of blasphemous names, and it had seven heads and ten horns. [4]The woman was clothed in purple and scarlet, and adorned with gold and jewels and pearls, holding in her hand a golden cup full of abominations and the impurities of her fornication; [5]and on her forehead was written a name, a mystery: "Babylon the great, mother of whores and of earth's abominations." [6]And I saw that the woman was drunk with the blood of the saints and the blood of the witnesses to Jesus.

When I saw her, I was greatly amazed. [7]But the angel said to me, "Why are you so amazed? I will tell you the mystery of the woman, and of the beast with seven heads and ten horns that carries her. [8]The beast that you saw was, and is not, and is about to ascend from the bottomless pit and go to destruction. And the inhabitants of the earth, whose names have not been written in the Book of Life from the foundation of the world, will be amazed when they see the beast, because it was and is not and is to come.

[9]"This calls for a mind that has wisdom: the seven heads are seven mountains on which the woman is seated; also, they are seven kings, [10]of whom five have fallen, one is living, and the other has not yet come; and when he comes, he must remain only a little

while. [11]As for the beast that was and is not, it is an eighth but it belongs to the seventh, and it goes to destruction. [12]And the ten horns that you saw are ten kings who have not yet received a kingdom, but they are to receive authority as kings for one hour, together with the beast. [13]These are united in yielding their power and authority to the beast; [14]they will make war on the Lamb, and the Lamb will conquer them, for he is Lord of lords and King of kings, and those with him are called and chosen and faithful."

[15]And he said to me, "The waters that you saw, where the whore is seated, are peoples and multitudes and nations and languages. [16]And the ten horns that you saw, they and the beast will hate the whore; they will make her desolate and naked; they will devour her flesh and burn her up with fire. [17]For God has put it into their hearts to carry out his purpose by agreeing to give their kingdom to the beast, until the words of God will be fulfilled. [18]The woman you saw is the great city that rules over the kings of the earth."

The Vision of the Harlot Seated upon the Beast (Rv 17:1-6)

An angel continues what has been described as the fall of Babylon (14:8; 16:9) by showing to John of Patmos a gaudy and almost comical depiction of a woman who is a monumental prostitute called "Babylon." She is seated upon the beast. John is recalling the effects of ancient Babylon when it conquered and ravaged Jewish peoples, destroyed their holy city of Jerusalem and led them into the Babylonian captivity. In this new "Babylon" the Roman Empire is doing the same to the witnesses of Jesus (the martyrs) and the churches (the people of God). Babylon is Rome. Passages from the Hebrew prophets about branding idolatrous cities as harlots must be ringing in the ears of the seer once the angel shows and explains this new phenomenon (See Is 23:16f; Na 3:4f), Israel (Ezk 16), Samaria and Jerusalem (Ezk 23).

"Prostitution" is equivalent to idolatry in the Bible and certainly that has been the intended meaning here in the Book of

Revelation. In describing the harlot, "Babylon," a threefold emphasis is made of her lusting behavior with the kings and peoples of the earth. I like to envision a contrast of this prostitute with the woman clothed with the sun who appears in the heavens (Rv 12:1-6). The separation between heaven and earth is evident; the same holds true for the woman representing in symbol the Church, and the opposite imaging of the woman riding on the beast above many waters and, yet, upon the earth. Both the Church and the cohorts of the whore will clash in the great battle on earth. The persecution has already started, but victory will be brought to the promised woman of Revelation 12.

The lavishness and sensuality of this whore of Babylon is a metaphor for the opulence, extravagance, and power of the Roman Empire extending over the waters of the Mediterranean up to the waters and canals in Babylon (Baghdad in modern Iraq). Upon the beast, which may be Nero returned to life, the prostitute rides over all earthly powers.

Settings are also important in understanding this vision. In the scene the seer is transported to the desert where he then sees and marvels at what the angel is pointing out to him. Desolation is implied in this desert setting. God is not present. Later, the visionary will be taken to a mountain where the New Jerusalem will be contemplated. Mountains are settings where God is to be found (Rv 21:10).

The woman prostitute is colossal in size riding like a goddess upon a monster — the beast. She is covered with the colors of Rome, scarlet mixed with regal purple. The vision is exotic, if not, erotic, for even John is tantalized by her splendor. She is tattooed with blasphemous names and branded with the sign or names of a prostitute on her forehead. I am reminded of the brothels at Pompeii, which are illuminated with vulgar and lustful commercials giving the number and style of the prostitute. One saintly priest was unwilling to let our tour group look at or enter these excavated houses of prostitution from the first century. In the mind of John, this is what the Roman Empire is all about.

At the time of the final redaction of Revelation, the Roman Emperors were claiming to be divine and eternal. Their idolatry was imposed upon all citizens; their buildings and public offices were inscribed with divine titles for the Roman Caesar. One such expression is ironically similar to a title reserved for God: "the one who was, who is, and who is to come."

The woman prostitute is given the name "Babylon the Great, the Mother of Harlots and Abominations of the Earth." John is struck with her amazing and colorful appearance, but is brought to his senses once he realizes that she is a metaphor for Rome and the beast (Nero, returned to life). It is she who is drunk with the blood of the holy prophets, the saints, and the martyrs of Jesus. John says, "I wondered with great wonder!" (Rv 17:6).

The Harlot Overthrown (Rv 17:7-13)

The angel now reveals the "mystery" of the woman carried by the beast. The combination of whore and beast is the mysterious symbol of Nero who represents the ultimate Antichrist for this epoch; he was somehow thought to be leading the Parthians' victory over the whole Roman Empire. He would come from the East, that is, from Babylon. His divine title indicates that he who ruled Rome in the first great persecution is dead, but now returns to life, becoming the present adversary of the Christians and an imposter of the ever living God. This is an abomination! The beast has emerged from the abyss and, therefore, is from the Devil.

An aside is given in verse 9 which enables the readers to realize that Rome is definitely meant; the seven heads are the seven mountains surrounding the city of Rome. Wisdom from God is necessary to decipher all of this, and it is given to John through the angel.

Verse 10 speaks of seven kings and one is yet to come. By listing emperors from Nero to Domitian one can arrive at the time period and come to the interpretation that the following emperors are meant:

1. Nero (54-68 C.E.)
2. Galba (68-69 C.E.)
3. Otho (69 C.E.)
4. Vitellius (69 C.E.)
5. Vespasian (69-79 C.E.)
6. Titus (79-81 C.E.)
7. Domitian (81-96 C.E.) = the legend of Nero returned to life and feared by the whole empire.

John may have used a source for verses 10-13 which indicated these emperors. However, the apocalyptic symbolism is not clear; this is part of the mysteriousness that both the visionary and we, the readers, experience.

If we tie together the former reference of 13:3: "One of its heads seemed to have received a death blow, but its mortal wound had been healed," with verse 11 of this chapter, it fits the emperor Nero who committed suicide in 68 C.E. and who now as a *redivivus* has returned.

The ten kings presented under the symbols of ten horns would represent lesser pro-consuls, governors, or rulers in the provinces of the Roman Empire. They are under the power of Rome and its emperor which is represented by the figure of the beast. Verse 14 lines up these "kings" in war against the Lamb. The ultimate battle between the followers of the beast and those of the Lamb is foretold. The Lamb will emerge with a more stunning victory than that of the great harlot riding the beast. The Lamb is Lord of lords and King of kings. The faithful followers of the Lamb are called and chosen to be victorious with him.

The title of both the whore and the Lamb represent this ultimate battle. In some Greek manuscripts both titles were capitalized demonstrating that they are mortal enemies. The title is therefore important for the reader to understand the symbolism of evil against good.

Is there a specific woman behind the symbolism of the harlot? Valeria Messalina, the wife of Claudius (41-54 C.E.) was put to death by her husband because of her notorious acts of lust and

harlotry. She could be the one who would typify what the visionary intends. It is possible that she is drunk with the blood of the
Christian martyrs who are the righteous offspring of the woman of
chapter 12. Mary of Nazareth is the only historical person who has
a possibility of being understood as the woman with offspring who
are righteous. On the bigger tableau of salvation history the symbolism can be understood as the worldly power of Rome against
the churches of early Christianity.

Verses 16 and 17 are two of the most dreadful in Revelation.
In the end evil destroys evil and gloats over its bloody and naked
victim, the harlot Rome. Here care is to be taken lest this negative image do further damage to women. It was a "man's world"
during the actual time of Revelation. It's use of feminine imagery
is quite violent in this chapter — probably the most violent in the
New Testament. Adele Yarbro Collins offers sound advice in interpreting such symbolism: "In the twentieth (and twenty-first)
century such images may not be used uncritically because, e.g., their
ill effects on the lives of women have been recognized" (*The Apocalypse, NJBC*, 1012).

A splendid display of the creative genius of the author is
manifested in the rich artistic description of chapter 18. In my es-
timation, this tripartite scene is the most poetic and colorful
example of rhetoric in all of Revelation. Pure poetry delights the
reader and listener as the prophetic taunt breaks forth: "Babylon,
the great and mighty city has fallen, has fallen." It is a powerful
judgmental dirge which haunts you as you experience the cadenced
rhythm of the lines. The Roman Empire is envisioned as seeing its
last days, yes, even its last hour.

Where did the visionary acquire this extraordinary description of how the mighty Babylon has fallen? It has its provenance
from the great literary masterpieces of Isaiah, Jeremiah, and Ezekiel
in their own God-given judgment over sinful cities and nations.
The seer has spent many hours in isolation possibly in the traditional site of the cave in which he lived. Genius springs from long
hours of contemplating the sacred writings; the prophetic dirges,

court scenes, and soliloquies of these holy authors have influenced our prophet John of Patmos. Nothing can stop him now in relating the vision given to him by a power-laden angel of light who opens the scene for us.

Food for the Journey:

Romans 1:28-32

> [28]And since they did not see fit to acknowledge God, God gave them up to a debased mind and to things that should not be done. [29]They were filled with every kind of wickedness, evil, covetousness, malice. Full of envy, murder, strife, deceit, craftiness, they are gossips, [30]slanderers, God-haters, insolent, haughty, boastful, inventors of evil, rebellious toward parents, [31]foolish, faithless, heartless, ruthless. [32]They know God's decree, that those who practice such things deserve to die — yet they not only do them but even applaud others who practice them.

Revelation 18:1-24

> [1]After this I saw another angel coming down from heaven, having great authority; and the earth was made bright with his splendor. [2]He called out with a mighty voice, "Fallen, fallen is Babylon the great! It has become a dwelling place of demons, a haunt of every foul spirit, a haunt of every foul bird, a haunt of every foul and hateful beast. [3]For all the nations have drunk of the wine of the wrath of her fornication, and the kings of the earth have committed fornication with her, and the merchants of the earth have grown rich from the power of her luxury." [4]Then I heard another voice from heaven saying, "Come out of her, my people, so that you do not take part in her sins, and so that you do not share in her plagues; [5]for her sins are heaped high as heaven, and God has remembered her iniquities. [6]Render to her as she herself has rendered, and repay her double for her deeds; mix a double draught for her in the cup she mixed. [7]As she glorified herself and

lived luxuriously, so give her a like measure of torment and grief. Since in her heart she says, 'I rule as a queen; I am no widow, and I will never see grief,' [8]therefore her plagues will come in a single day — pestilence and mourning and famine — and she will be burned with fire; for mighty is the Lord God who judges her."

[9]And the kings of the earth, who committed fornication and lived in luxury with her, will weep and wail over her when they see the smoke of her burning; [10]they will stand far off, in fear of her torment, and say, "Alas, alas, the great city, Babylon, the mighty city! For in one hour your judgment has come."

[11]And the merchants of the earth weep and mourn for her, since no one buys their cargo anymore, [12]cargo of gold, silver, jewels and pearls, fine linen, purple, silk and scarlet, all kinds of scented wood, all articles of ivory, all articles of costly wood, bronze, iron, and marble, [13]cinnamon, spice, incense, myrrh, frankincense, wine, olive oil, choice flour and wheat, cattle and sheep, horses and chariots, slaves — and human lives.

[14]"The fruit for which your soul longed has gone from you, and all your dainties and your splendor are lost to you, never to be found again!"

[15]The merchants of these wares, who gained wealth from her, will stand far off, in fear of her torment, weeping and mourning aloud, [16]"Alas, alas, the great city, clothed in fine linen, in purple and scarlet, adorned with gold, with jewels, and with pearls! [17]For in one hour all this wealth has been laid waste!" And all shipmasters and seafarers, sailors and all whose trade is on the sea, stood far off [18]and cried out as they saw the smoke of her burning, "What city was like the great city?" [19]And they threw dust on their heads, as they wept and mourned, crying out, "Alas, alas, the great city, where all who had ships at sea grew rich by her wealth! For in one hour she has been laid waste. [20]Rejoice over her, O heaven, you saints and apostles and prophets! For God has given judgment for you against her."

[21]Then a mighty angel took up a stone like a great millstone and threw it into the sea, saying, "With such violence Babylon the great city will be thrown down, and will be found no more; [22]and the sound of harpists and minstrels and of flutists and trum-

peters will be heard in you no more; and an artisan of any trade will be found in you no more; and the sound of the millstone will be heard in you no more; [23]and the light of a lamp will shine in you no more; and the voice of bridegroom and bride will be heard in you no more; for your merchants were the magnates of the earth, and all nations were deceived by your sorcery. [24]And in you was found the blood of prophets and of saints, and of all who have been slaughtered on earth."

The Fall of Babylon (Rome) and God's Judgment (Rv 18:1-8)

John experiences another vision which continues and completes what he just saw. An angel of light announces the fall of Babylon which then becomes the prison of demons and all that is associated with filthiness, that is, evil. The strong voice of the angel declares, "Babylon the mighty has fallen, has fallen."

This announcement is reinforced by another voice and prophetical oracle in 18:4-5 and 18:6-8. The condemnatory sentence is upon the kings and nations who have committed fornication (idolatry) with the woman in scarlet. The wrath (judgment) of God is upon those who have enjoyed the pleasures of the empire and continued to exploit and oppress the poor and have murdered the holy ones of God on this earth. The angelic voice advises those who are faithful to make their exodus from the city which is about to be destroyed.

God's judgment is just. The sins of Babylon have been remembered. How could God not notice them? They reach as high as the heavens in their enormity and cruelty.

A new Exodus is being called for, only this time God's people are to leave aside all of the riches, the jewelry and the pleasures offered by Babylon. Haste is important for all will happen in a day; yes, even in an hour! God's people are to give back all they may have received from the harlot and the beast. Give it back doubly for the time is short. By so doing, no plague or sorrow will be felt by the faithful. Do not be trapped by the luxuries and idolatries of the nations and kings who have worshiped this false goddess, Rome, and the beast.

Elisabeth Schüssler Fiorenza has brilliantly researched the structure of this chapter. She states: "Chapter 18 not only constitutes the middle panel within the overall triptych of 17:1-19:10. It also is composed like a triptych within a triptych. Two proclamations of judgment (18:1-8 and 21-24) frame the series of dirges (18:9-19) that, in turn, are again composed in a tripartite fashion. The kings' lament (18:9-10) and that of the ship owners (18:17-19) frame the central lament of the merchants (18:11-16). The whole sequence forms an artful literary composition whose nestling technique could be compared to a Russian doll containing several other dolls. John achieves a strong unitary composition with imaginative power, although he derives the language and imagery of this section almost verbatim from divergent sources. His artistic skill proves itself in the interweaving of various, often contradictory, traditions into a unified composition with great rhetorical power" (*Revelation*: Proclamation Series, Fortress, Minneapolis, 1991, pp. 98-99).

St. Augustine in his *City of God* (18:18) has a statement which captures the spiritual meaning of this new Exodus: "The prophetic command is to be understood spiritually; we are to flee this earthly city, setting out for God with the steps of faith."

Christians were impressed by the opulence and luxury of the Roman Empire. We remember the warnings given to them in the scroll sent to the seven churches. They, undoubtedly, experience some sadness in the prophetic declaration that this empire is soon to come to an end. The angel's revelation to John is telling him to have the faithful followers of the Lamb (Jesus now glorified in heaven) continue their consistent resistance to the power, riches, and sensuality of the rulers of this earth. Already many who have witnessed Jesus have been slaughtered. God will not leave murderers unpunished. These Christians are to be watchful, for the alluring glitter of possessions is always tempting and can thwart their liberation from the oppressors.

Even though Babylon is on the verge of total destruction she has her own poetic soliloquy saying she is a queen and not a widow. In the Book of Judges the mother of Sisera had a similar boastful poem thinking that her son was returning in victory as she peered out of her window. Her ladies in attendance were telling her that Sisera is probably dividing the spoils. In reality she is a widow without a husband, without a son. Deborah closes the song offsetting the queen's soliloquy: "So perish all your enemies, O lord! But may your friends be like the sun as it rises in its might." Babylon's vain refrain is just as empty and worthless as that of Sisera's mother (v. 7). God's judgment is righteous and effective. In an hour (a short time) Babylon will be sentenced to plagues, sorrow, famine, and even death. Conflagration will be the final stroke of God's strong judgment. Nero's burning of the city will be nothing in comparison to this final fire of God's justice.

The Dirge of the Kings, Merchants, and Seafarers (Rv 18:9-19)

Three dramatic woes are expressed in this section with each of the peoples who have profited from worshiping the beast and who have participated in the prostitution of the woman. They gaze on from a distance and wail for the burning and torments of their master and mistress. The woes are cadenced and rhythmical in the original language of the text. A definite mood of extreme bereavement accompanies them and heightens the drama of the distant city and empire which burn with unquenchable fires: "Woe! Woe! the great city, the strong metropolis of Babylon has fallen and undergone God's just verdict in one hour." The merchants wail, for no longer can they sell their precious cargo.

The list of 29 precious products are presented in staccato tempo. The Greek words flow one into another with a certain and beautiful cadence demonstrating what a great loss these merchants are suffering.

The seer is undoubtedly recalling similar dirges about Tyre and its merchants who are described in Ezekiel and Isaiah (see Is 24:21-23; Ezk 27:12-25). The allusions are spread throughout this chapter reminding us of how God's prophetic word was pondered and remembered by John of Patmos.

The losses continue to be enumerated including livestock, horses, beasts of burden. By the expression "bodies and souls" slaves are meant.

The next woe bellows out from their once ravenous throats as more goods and riches are enumerated. Such sumptuous wealth is worthless without the beast and the prostitute called Babylon. All has become desolate as a desert as the end comes near in the total conflagration of the city and its provinces.

The merchant marines and seafarers join in the lamentation as the death knoll is sounded in the final woe of the dirge of doom. These latter are so stunned by the devastation that they throw ashes over their heads in lamentation as they express this climactic woe. How could the great city fall? How was this possible?

The Saints, Apostles, and Prophets Rejoice at the Judgment of Babylon (Rv 18:20-24)

As the dirge over Babylon ends, an exhortatory paean of joy summons the heavens, the holy ones, prophets, and apostles to rejoice over God's judgment upon Babylon. To demonstrate the complete destruction of the unholy city, an angel throws a great millstone into the sea as a prophetic action illustrating the annihilation of Babylon. This image is an allusion to Jeremiah's symbolic action which demonstrated the fall of historic Babylon over 600 years earlier: "When you finish reading this scroll, tie a stone to it, and throw it into the middle of the Euphrates and say, 'Thus shall Babylon sink, to rise no more, because of the disaster that I am bringing to her'" (Jr 51:63-64).

All that is associated with the Roman Empire's glory and power will then be silenced. No more music from the harpists, trumpeters, and flutists; no more shops; not even the sound of a grain mill will remain. Wedding celebrations are heard never again. Why? Because the merchants and magistrates had impoverished the peoples and slaughtered the holy ones and the prophets.

The judgment of God upon the evils of Roman civilization has vindicated the innocent blood of the faithful. What the seer has done for us is to show how greed, violence, oppression, and exploitation have undermined what Rome thought to be its glory. We are about to see a reversal of all these atrocities as the next scene opens.

Food for the Journey:

Jeremiah 51:6-10

> [6]Flee from the midst of Babylon, save your lives, each of you! Do not perish because of her guilt, for this is the time of the Lord's vengeance; he is repaying her what is due. [7]Babylon was a golden cup in the Lord's hand, making all the earth drunken; the nations drank of her wine, and so the nations went mad. [8]Suddenly Babylon has fallen and is shattered; wail for her! Bring balm for her wound; perhaps she may be healed. [9]We tried to heal Babylon, but she could not be healed. Forsake her, and let each of us go to our own country; for her judgment has reached up to heaven and has been lifted up even to the skies. [10]The Lord has brought forth our vindication; come, let us declare in Zion the work of the Lord our God.

CHAPTER SEVEN

THE END OF EVIL AND THE BEGINNING OF THE NEW JERUSALEM
(Rv 19-22)

Revelation 19:1-21

¹After this I heard what seemed to be the loud voice of a great multitude in heaven, saying, "Hallelujah! Salvation and glory and power to our God, ²for his judgments are true and just; he has judged the great whore who corrupted the earth with her fornication, and he has avenged on her the blood of his servants." ³Once more they said, "Hallelujah! The smoke goes up from her forever and ever." ⁴And the twenty-four elders and the four living creatures fell down and worshiped God who is seated on the throne, saying, "Amen. Hallelujah!" ⁵And from the throne came a voice saying, "Praise our God, all you his servants, and all who fear him, small and great."

⁶Then I heard what seemed to be the voice of a great multitude, like the sound of many waters and like the sound of mighty thunder peals, crying out, "Hallelujah! For the Lord our God the Almighty reigns. ⁷Let us rejoice and exult and give him the glory, for the marriage of the Lamb has come, and his bride has made herself ready; ⁸to her it has been granted to be clothed with fine linen, bright and pure" — for the fine linen is the righteous deeds of the saints. ⁹And the angel said to me, "Write this: Blessed are those who are invited to the marriage supper of the Lamb." And he said to me, "These are true words of God."

[10]Then I fell down at his feet to worship him, but he said to me, "You must not do that! I am a fellow servant with you and your comrades who hold the testimony of Jesus. Worship God! For the testimony of Jesus is the spirit of prophecy."

[11]Then I saw heaven opened, and there was a white horse! Its rider is called Faithful and True, and in righteousness he judges and makes war. [12]His eyes are like a flame of fire, and on his head are many diadems; and he has a name inscribed that no one knows but himself. [13]He is clothed in a robe dipped in blood, and his name is called The Word of God. [14]And the armies of heaven, wearing fine linen, white and pure, were following him on white horses. [15]From his mouth comes a sharp sword with which to strike down the nations, and he will rule them with a rod of iron; he will tread the wine press of the fury of the wrath of God the Almighty. [16]On his robe and on his thigh he has a name inscribed, "King of kings and Lord of lords."

[17]Then I saw an angel standing in the sun, and with a loud voice he called to all the birds that fly in midheaven, "Come, gather for the great supper of God, [18]to eat the flesh of kings, the flesh of captains, the flesh of the mighty, the flesh of horses and their riders — flesh of all, both free and slave, both small and great."

[19]Then I saw the beast and the kings of the earth with their armies gathered to make war against the rider on the horse and against his army. [20]And the beast was captured, and with it the false prophet who had performed in its presence the signs by which he deceived those who had received the mark of the beast and those who worshiped its image. These two were thrown alive into the lake of fire that burns with sulfur. [21]And the rest were killed by the sword of the rider on the horse, the sword that came from his mouth; and all the birds were gorged with their flesh.

John of Patmos speaks:

Finally, my own vision became more pleasing to the eye and I heard a message soothing to the ear for something great was to be celebrated. Is there any celebration more beautiful than a wedding and a wedding banquet? Amidst the Amens! and Alleluias, came the message "Let us rejoice and be glad and give glory to the Lord God the Almighty (*Pantocrator*), for the marriage of the lamb has come. His bride has made herself ready."

Then Jesus, the Lamb, was now a handsome rider called Faithful and True. He was the Word of God and the truth from his mouth was a sharp sword. He was the bridegroom and the victor who by his own precious blood avenged the blood of the saints. Evil was overcome by this princely figure.

The beast and the kings of the earth mustered forces against him. They were as numerous as the sands on the seashore. To my amazement they never really engaged in a final battle against Jesus the King of kings and Lord of lords. His truth and fidelity called their bluff — they were no more than their leader, the devil or the dragon. Lies, deceit, and shameful practices were suddenly bound up, for Satan was thrown into the abyss and locked therein. I understood it to be for a long period of time and then he would be freed to try once more for a final Armageddon. He was again vanquished by the truth of God's Word and bound up forever. Those who were his followers experienced what I called the second death, that is, they were judged and thrown into the burning lake of sulfur. Death and Hades likewise were thrown into this lake.

Scrolls were opened in heaven and the names of the martyrs, the prophets, and the holy ones were read from a special scroll called the "Book of Life." Those whose names were not inscribed therein experienced the second death.

Then I saw a new heaven and a new earth. God had promised to make all things new. I saw the glorious splendor and dazzling beauty of the bride of the Lamb. She was as wonderfully adorned as the holy city of Jerusalem. I felt great peace and joy as I looked at her and remembered the covenant God had made with humankind. God was our parent and we God's children. The Bride of the Lamb is the Church and she is loved by Jesus. How I wished we would understand such love and fidelity.

I was almost out of my senses as an angel with a gold measuring rod summoned me to look at the New Jerusalem. Every precious stone I could think of was within its walls. Gold, crystal, and pearls brightened the city of God. There was no temple; there was no need for sunlight, nor the light from the moon. The glory of God was its light and its lamp was the Lamb. Down the middle of the city was a crystal clear river which flowed with the waters of life and nourished the trees planted on each side. Each month of the year, the trees yielded fruit and a healing balm was in their leaves.

I was deeply moved and filled with confidence in my role as servant-prophet of God, the Alpha and Omega, the beginning and the end. I heard the angel say, "These words are trustworthy and true. The Lord God who inspires the prophets has sent his angel to show his servants what must soon take place."

I, John of Patmos, tell you that all I have experienced is true and trustworthy. If you ask me what the greatest message for the churches, for you, and for me is in this revelation, I would say, "Worship God!" I was encouraged not to seal anything in this scroll but to reveal it.

How more consoled I was as the prophesy and vision were ending. Jesus himself now addressed me: "I, Jesus, have sent my angel to give you this testimony for the churches. I am the root and offspring of David, the bright morning star." And Jesus ended this revelation with a promise: "Yes, I am coming soon!" I broke down in tears, fell on my knees and prayed in my native language of Aramaic, "Amen! Maranatha Jeshoua! Come, Lord Jesus. Amen." And, my brothers and sisters, may the grace of the Lord Jesus be with us all.

COMMENTARY

A Glimpse into the Heavenly Worship and Praise of God (Rv 19:1-10)

Counterpoised to offset the gruesome and violent scenes which took place in chapter 18, the visionary now experiences the heavens opening and he hears the songs and exclamations of praise offered to God seated upon a throne. This is not the first time that we have seen the narrator giving us such contemplative and joyous descriptions of the heavenly court after destructive and negative events have just been narrated.

A great crowd is worshiping God in heaven singing four Alleluias. This Hebrew word expresses the entire message of the book — "Worship God!" "Praise God!" Literally, the Hebrew means, "Praise Yah (Yahweh)." It is used in the liturgical worship of the temple in Jerusalem at the beginning and sometimes at the end of Psalms (Ps 111-117); Ps 150 is one big Alleluia! In the New Testament the word Alleluia is found only in Revelation in chapter 19 (vv. 1,3,4, and 6). This shout of praise is being proclaimed constantly by the heavenly elect to celebrate the victory of God's final triumph.

The heart of praising God at this point in the narrative is the salvation, glory, and power of "our" God. The plural possessive pronoun links those in heaven with the seer and the churches of the faithful on earth. In a Catholic perspective, this is the Communion of Saints offering praise to God and a model in heaven for those on earth who are called to honor God with adoration and intercession. This union has been based on the paschal mysteries of the Lamb of God and sustained through the faith and worship of the witnesses to Jesus on earth. It is a union without confusion; a *koinônia* or community of brothers and sisters united with what is happening in the heavenly realm before the throne of God. Those who have gone before us in faith are with the angels, the apostles, and the prophets united in chorus before God.

We may wonder whether there is vengeance in God's justice on behalf of the martyrs of both covenants, the first in the Hebrew Scriptures and the covenant enacted upon Calvary through the death of Jesus. Does this vengeful dimension of God go beyond what the Gospels tell us? Or is it, as A. Yarbro Collins points out, a catharsis for those who feel oppressed and powerless before the kings and mighty ones of the earthly empires, helping them to sense that God is on their side and the victory of Jesus will bring them through this time of trial and crisis here on earth?

A reading of this chapter would lead us to believe that Jesus' victory over evil and death in all of its manifest forms overcomes the rejection and marginalization the faithful have experienced in the Roman Empire.

The second Alleluia chorus celebrates this great victory in the conflagration of the harlot city.

Next, the four living creatures reaffirm the Alleluia with an Amen while worshiping the living God who is, was, and will be. Every facet of Rome's power and pride is offset by what now is happening in the heavenly court.

Another voice summons all in the heavens (and on earth?) to praise God. Another great crowd (is it the 144,000 or the innumerable peoples, languages, and nations of saints?) whose voices are so numerous that they resemble the sound of many deep waters and waterfalls — thunderous echoes of more peoples saying "Alleluia. God is our King, the Almighty One."

Something new is to happen. The Lamb is preparing himself for his bride. The heavenly assembly rejoices at the pre-nuptial announcement. In fact, the bride who is the universal Church is preparing herself for the wedding banquet. Her wedding gown is of pure white linen which symbolically means the holiness and faithfulness of the individual churches.

The angel then tells John to write the truthful words of God which are another macarism or beatitude: "Blessed are those who are invited to the marriage supper of the Lamb."

This vision is so breathtaking that our visionary, John of

Patmos, falls at the feet of the angel and almost worships him. The messenger prevents this mistake with a gentle reprimand, but probably with a smile, while reminding John that he, too, is a servant and one of the community of worshipers who has the testimony of Jesus which is to worship only God. This is what the prophesy is concerned with, namely, the worship of God.

Christ the Victor (Rv 19:11-16)

Handel's "Messiah" has captured in classical music the power of this passage. A further development of the Christology of Revelation appears, and, it is good to keep both the Alleluia Chorus of the Messiah as background music as well as to realize that a magnificent title is given to Jesus: He is King of kings and Lord of lords as the section ends. I have already mentioned that many of the Greek manuscripts which are written in minuscule (script) are converted into uncials (Greek capital letters) for this particular titular verse 19.

White is the color of victory as well as of holiness in the symbolic schema of Revelation. Jesus manifests himself in splendid fashion riding upon a white horse. Jesus is the rider named Faithful and True. We are reminded of the Prologue of John's Gospel where Jesus is described as the Father's only son, full of grace and truth (Jn 1:14c). Jesus is judge and warrior in a holy battle against the forces of evil.

The figure of Jesus' face is overpowering, for his eyes are burning like flames of fire and his mouth opens with a sharp sword of truth, while his name is mysteriously known only to himself, but, ironically revealed as the Word of God. We are at the heart of the Christology revealed to us by the seer. It is consistent with the Johannine tradition of the Fourth Gospel, only the image of warfare is different. His garment is dipped in blood and yet, paradoxically, is a brilliant white linen. It may symbolize the blood that he shed on the cross for the washing and freeing of all humankind or it may symbolize the blood of the martyrs.

Jesus is followed by an army troop mounted on white horses and clothed in white linen garments like his own. The sword from his mouth is the truth of his judgment and decision over the nations. A messianic Psalm is alluded to as he is said to shepherd the same nations with an iron rod (Ps 2:8-9, already seen in Rv 12:5). One also is led to think of Psalm 45, an ode for a royal wedding. In the extended context of chapter 19 we are aware of the wedding preparations for the Lamb and his bride: "You are the most handsome of men; grace is poured out upon your lips; therefore God has blessed you forever. Gird your sword on your thigh, O mighty one, in your glory and majesty. In your majesty ride on victoriously for the cause of truth and to defend the right; let your right hand teach you valorous deeds. Your Arrows are sharp in the heart of the kings' enemies; the people fall under you" (Ps 45:2-5).

The victorious one also treads the winepress of God's wrath. Perhaps, here the symbolism of the blood of the grape is for human blood that is being exacted by God for the shedding of the innocent blood of the holy ones, the prophets, and the apostles. The victory march ends with the banner of the rider displayed upon his thighs: "King of kings and Lord of lords" (v. 16).

The End of Evil (Rv 19:17-21)

Another angel is standing in the sun — a symbol of God surrounding someone. In a bizarre scene all flying creatures are invited to gather at the wedding banquet in order to feast on the carcasses of those slain: kings, captains, warriors and all of their cavalry as well as their slaves and servants. Again such bloody scenes refer to the profound catharsis of those who have been exploited and appeased — the poor and the marginal.

The dreaded beast and all of the regents of the empire gather their forces to meet the rider of the white horse and his armies. The stage is set for the battle of good against evil; heaven against earth; Christ against Satan and his beast.

Both the beast and the false prophet are quickly dispatched.

They had deceived so many with their idolatry and their images that vengeance is mercilessly thrust upon them. Both are thrown into a lake of fire burning with sulfur. Their armies, as well as their contingents, are likewise killed with the sword of truth coming from Christ's mouth. The chapter ends with the birds of heaven feasting like vultures on their flesh. In one hour the cohorts of the prince of darkness have been defeated. Evil has come to an end.

Food for the Journey:

Psalm 45:1-45:7

> [1]My heart overflows with a goodly theme; I address my verses to the king; my tongue is like the pen of a ready scribe. [2]You are the most handsome of men; grace is poured upon your lips; therefore God has blessed you forever. [3]Gird your sword on your thigh, O mighty one, in your glory and majesty. [4]In your majesty ride on victoriously for the cause of truth and to defend the right; let your right hand teach you dread deeds. [5]Your arrows are sharp in the heart of the king's enemies; the peoples fall under you. [6]Your throne, O God, endures forever and ever. Your royal scepter is a scepter of equity; [7]you love righteousness and hate wickedness. Therefore God, your God, has anointed you with the oil of gladness beyond your companions; [8]your robes are all fragrant with myrrh and aloes and cassia. From ivory palaces stringed instruments make you glad.

Revelation 20:1-15

> [1]Then I saw an angel coming down from heaven, holding in his hand the key to the bottomless pit and a great chain. [2]He seized the dragon, that ancient serpent, who is the Devil and Satan, and bound him for a thousand years, [3]and threw him into the pit, and locked and sealed it over him, so that he would deceive the nations no more, until the thousand years were ended. After that he must be let out for a little while.

[4]Then I saw thrones, and those seated on them were given authority to judge. I also saw the souls of those who had been beheaded for their testimony to Jesus and for the word of God. They had not worshiped the beast or its image and had not received its mark on their foreheads or their hands. They came to life and reigned with Christ a thousand years. [5](The rest of the dead did not come to life until the thousand years were ended.) This is the first resurrection. [6]Blessed and holy are those who share in the first resurrection. Over these the second death has no power, but they will be priests of God and of Christ, and they will reign with him a thousand years.

[7]When the thousand years are ended, Satan will be released from his prison [8]and will come out to deceive the nations at the four corners of the earth, Gog and Magog, in order to gather them for battle; they are as numerous as the sands of the sea. [9]They marched up over the breadth of the earth and surrounded the camp of the saints and the beloved city. And fire came down from heaven and consumed them. [10]And the devil who had deceived them was thrown into the lake of fire and sulfur, where the beast and the false prophet were, and they will be tormented day and night forever and ever.

[11]Then I saw a great white throne and the one who sat on it; the earth and the heavens fled from his presence, and no place was found for them. [12]And I saw the dead, great and small, standing before the throne, and books were opened. Also another book was opened, the book of life. And the dead were judged according to their works, as recorded in the books. [13]And the sea gave up the dead that were in it, Death and Hades gave up the dead that were in them, and all were judged according to what they had done. [14]Then Death and Hades were thrown into the lake of fire. This is the second death, the lake of fire; [15]and anyone whose name was not found written in the Book of Life was thrown into the lake of fire.

The End of Satan (Rv 20:1-10)

In this chapter eschatology (the last events and judgments) and ecclesiology (the gathering and community of the faithful) are intertwined. Our narrator has a penchant for repeating the themes of the vision. There is also a web-like connection in these final chapters where words, images, and phrases knit together in his weave-like literary style. What is lacking in syntax and grammar is compensated for in the artistic imagery and creative inventiveness of the author. We are well aware of the manner in which the narrator returns to the beginning of the vision in the initial chapter and of how the message to the seven churches keeps coming back to us as the visions and scenes unfold. This is a type of recapitulation that the writer favors somewhat similar to what Irenaeus will do some hundred years later.

Let us return to the theme of this chapter — the final judgment upon Satan, the beast, and the pseudo-prophet. The scene is still a continuation of chapter 19 introduced by a simple connecting phrase, "And I saw...." It is an angel who descends from the heavens and locks up Satan in the great abyss. He, Satan, is the one who has symbolic names such as the dragon, the ancient serpent and the devil. Satan is the real source of evil. He is thrown into the abysmal pit and bound up with chains. In a manner of speaking, he has been signed, sealed, and delivered to Hades.

His sentence to solitary confinement is a stiff one consisting of 1000 years. After that time (symbolic of a long period), Satan will be released. This leads us as readers into the perplexing problem of millennialism that has divided Christian believers and interpreters for ages as they offer their understanding of this isolated reference in the New Testament to a thousand year interim in which Christ will reign with the faithful witnesses of the Word of God, the martyrs of both testaments (Old Testament and New).

The concept of messianic millennialism stems from late Judaic apocalyptic literature (I Enoch, Baruch Apocalypse, 4th Ezra). There are clear parallel ideas to the Book of Revelation in I Enoch. In the continuing tradition of Christianity several early commentators were literal advocates of millennialism. Papias, Justin, Irenaeus, Tertullian and Hippolytus are among these literalists who taught such a thousand year reign of Christ.

Millennialism understood in this Book of Revelation affirms that after a first resurrection of the ones who were martyred, Christ would come to rule on earth in a period of peace for the faithful Christians for 1000 years. One only has to go to a local book store to find that many new titles appear each year on the shelves emphasizing this tendentious teaching. Even in the twenty-first century, a certain hysteria sets in with focus on Israel and its capital Jerusalem, or on technology's struggle with its own symbolic "666" — the ever present "zero." As early as 1944 the teaching office of the Catholic Church pronounced that a form of 'mitigated millennialism' should not be taught. This referred to the temporary reign of Christ here on earth for a period of 1000 years before the final judgment. (AAS 36 [1944], 212). Father Raymond Brown in his last statement about the issues surrounding this doctrine wisely says, "The author of Revelation did not know how or when the world would end, and neither does anyone else" (*Introduction to the New Testament*, p. 810).

No modern prophet or self-claimed prophet has had one of their predictions from the Book of Revelation come true. Here in the United States we have been exposed to such millennialism since John Nelson Darby in 1840 who had to keep changing his end-time dates up to his own death. The same may be said for such prophetic authors in this and the last century (1800-1999). It is helpful to remember what Jesus says in the Acts of the Apostles: "It is not for you to know the times or periods that the Father has set by his own authority.... Be my witnesses... to the ends of the earth" (Ac 1:7-8).

The Millennial Rule of Christ (Rv 20:4-6)

In addition to the violent scenes in this inspired work, the present passage is among the most troublesome. It raises issues that I have touched upon above.

The pericope is understood as the first judgment dependent upon the first resurrection experienced by those who were beheaded for their witness to Christ. These martyrs are those who are seated upon thrones and are judging with authority those who have chosen Satan, the beast, its image and its mark and oppressed the poor and slaughtered the witnesses who now enjoy resurrected lives with the Christ. The martyrs seem to be the only ones from among the dead who experience this first resurrection. The rest of the dead must wait 1000 years before they face the final judgment of God, Christ, and the faithful witnesses.

In the theology of Revelation the martyrs are given a special place in the heavens. It is they who will judge the nations. Within a hundred years this idealism and ideology will invade the minds and hearts of Christians in Carthage who will long for, pray for, and even search out martyrdom. Origen in the third century sought to emulate his own father who was a martyr for the Church in Africa. There will always be such "martyr souls" and "martyr complexes" in the Church. Did this spirituality of martyrdom begin with Revelation?

One of the rewards given to the beheaded martyrs of Revelation is the fifth beatitude in Revelation: "Blessed and holy are those who share in the first resurrection" (v. 6).

The Final Defeat of Satan (Rv 20:7-10)

This passage is depicted in mythical language and centers on the final battle of the Devil against God's faithful people. Yet, we know the victory of Christ the Paschal Lamb is complete. This is but a recapitulation of what has already happened in chapter 19.

Is it that the battles take place between phantom armies of the dead? To indicate that God is ever present and in control of all history, whether cosmic or earthly, our writer makes use of the "divine passive voice" to announce Satan's defeat. Satan's cameo appearance has him scurrying to the four corners of the earth to release his already moribund troops. They are personified as being led by Gog and Magog — words taken from Ezekiel, cc. 37 and 38. Numerous as the sands of the sea they surround the camp of the saints and their holy city (Jerusalem). But ironically just as the false prophet has brought down fire from heaven, now God destroys these battalions of Satan with fire from heaven. The great deceiver and liar, the Devil, is now thrown into the lake of fire and sulfur where he will be tormented forever. No ultimate battle is waged, but prophecy and judgment are accomplished with a total defeat of the Devil.

The Dead Are Judged (Rv 20: 11-15)

Our final passage in this chapter is a contrast between death and life; between salvation and condemnation to the realm of the Devil known as the lake of fire. The scene opens with one seated upon a white throne — either God or Jesus. If the latter, we are led to remember him as the victorious rider on the white horse. In the Hebrew Scriptures there is a fear of dying should one see the face of God. This thought is also in our passage here, for both earth and all that is on it and the heavens or skies flee from the face of the one seated on the white throne. There is no place for them in the realm of God.

An assembly of those who have died are standing before the throne which also is the judgment seat of God. Scrolls or books are opened which have recorded the deeds of the dead. There is also the scroll of life which contains the names of the faithful witnesses. All of the dead are called forth from the sea and from the underworld. It is the final judgment and those not found in the

Book of Life experience what is called the second death. The writer tells us this is the lake of fire. Death and Hades, now personified, are thrown into the lake of fire.

Is this "second death" the final judgment or eternal damnation as expressed in traditional thought, or is it the judgment of those whose names are not in the Book of Life and are annihilated in the lake of fire? Both of these concepts are horrendous and frightening and are the equivalent of what we understand hell to be.

The call of the God we believe in is to choose life and not death. Here our own free will and our responsibility to choose life are the message the visionary receives for those who are witnesses to the word of God and to Jesus. The message is challenging and hopeful.

Food for the Journey:

Gaudium et Spes, #39 and #40

> Far from diminishing our concern to develop this earth, the expectancy of a new earth should spur us on, for it is here that the body of a new human family grows, foreshadowing in some way the age which is to come. That is why, although we must be careful to distinguish earthly progress clearly from the increase of the kingdom of Christ, such progress is of vital concern to the kingdom of God, insofar as it can contribute to the better ordering of human society.
>
> In pursing its own salvific purpose, not only does the Church communicate divine life to us, but in a certain sense, it casts the reflected light of that divine life over all the earth, notably in the way it heals and elevates the dignity of the human person in the way it consolidates society, and endows our daily activity with a deeper sense and meaning.

Revelation 21:1-27

¹Then I saw a new heaven and a new earth; for the first heaven and the first earth had passed away, and the sea was no more. ²And I saw the holy city, the new Jerusalem, coming down out of heaven from God, prepared as a bride adorned for her husband. ³And I heard a loud voice from the throne saying, "See, the home of God is among mortals. He will dwell with them as their God; they will be his peoples, and God himself will be with them; ⁴he will wipe every tear from their eyes. Death will be no more; mourning and crying and pain will be no more, for the first things have passed away."

⁵And the one who was seated on the throne said, "See, I am making all things new." Also he said, "Write this, for these words are trustworthy and true." ⁶Then he said to me, "It is done! I am the Alpha and the Omega, the beginning and the end. To the thirsty I will give water as a gift from the spring of the water of life. ⁷Those who conquer will inherit these things, and I will be their God and they will be my children. ⁸But as for the cowardly, the faithless, the polluted, the murderers, the fornicators, the sorcerers, the idolaters, and all liars, their place will be in the lake that burns with fire and sulfur, which is the second death."

⁹Then one of the seven angels who had the seven bowls full of the seven last plagues came and said to me, "Come, I will show you the bride, the wife of the Lamb." ¹⁰And in the spirit he carried me away to a great, high mountain and showed me the holy city Jerusalem coming down out of heaven from God. ¹¹It has the glory of God and a radiance like a very rare jewel, like jasper, clear as crystal. ¹²It has a great, high wall with twelve gates, and at the gates twelve angels, and on the gates are inscribed the names of the twelve tribes of the Israelites; ¹³on the east three gates, on the north three gates, on the south three gates, and on the west three gates. ¹⁴And the wall of the city has twelve foundations, and on them are the twelve names of the twelve apostles of the Lamb.

¹⁵The angel who talked to me had a measuring rod of gold to measure the city and its gates and walls. ¹⁶The city lies foursquare, its length the same as its width; and he measured the city

with his rod, fifteen hundred miles; its length and width and height are equal. [17]He also measured its wall, one hundred forty-four cubits by human measurement, which the angel was using. [18]The wall is built of jasper, while the city is pure gold, clear as glass. [19]The foundations of the wall of the city are adorned with every jewel; the first was jasper, the second sapphire, the third agate, the fourth emerald, [20]the fifth onyx, the sixth carnelian, the seventh chrysolite, the eighth beryl, the ninth topaz, the tenth chrysoprase, the eleventh jacinth, the twelfth amethyst. [21]And the twelve gates are twelve pearls, each of the gates is a single pearl, and the street of the city is pure gold, transparent as glass.

[22]I saw no temple in the city, for its temple is the Lord God the Almighty and the Lamb. [23]And the city has no need of sun or moon to shine on it, for the glory of God is its light, and its lamp is the Lamb. [24]The nations will walk by its light, and the kings of the earth will bring their glory into it. [25]Its gates will never be shut by day — and there will be no night there. [26]People will bring into it the glory and the honor of the nations. [27]But nothing unclean will enter it, nor anyone who practices abomination or falsehood, but only those who are written in the Lamb's book of life.

COMMENTARY

The New Heaven and the New Earth (Rv 21:1-8)

Our visionary experiences a breath of fresh air which leads him into the kaleidoscopic beauty of the new heaven and the new earth. It is a vision of the holy city of Jerusalem from above which also is the metaphor or image used for the bride of the Lamb, the Church. This is the most mystical section of the Book of Revelation and the most comforting of all revelations. Death, evil, darkness, and Satan with his cohorts, are no longer a part of the narration. We are experiencing with John of Patmos one of the most beautiful descriptions of heaven or the afterlife in all the New Testament. It will surpass all of the precious merchandise and luxuries offered by the Roman Empire and its extravagant civilization.

All things are made new by God. The covenantal love and God's fidelity are assurances that the faithful ones are now at complete peace; they are enjoying the glory of God in the golden pavements of heaven.

John sees a new creation of heaven and earth; all of the chaos that has been experienced is gone. Just as the first creation was expressed by the priestly tradition as being very good after each day, here in the Apocalypse all of the new creation will be aesthetically beautiful in a mystical description that has never been surpassed. The sea, which symbolizes chaos, is no longer. John is now letting out all the stops as he experiences what heaven is and how beautifully the bride of the Lamb is adorned.

Jerusalem, another name for the destiny of the Church, descends from the heavens as a bride who is prepared for her wedding. The voice of a revelatory angel declares that this is the *Shekinah*, the holy presence of God with the people of God, the Church. A covenantal relationship similar to that which Jeremiah had prophesied is now a reality: God dwells within the Church and its members are God's people. The theological thought is incarnational as well as covenantal for it resonates with the revelatory word of the Fourth Gospel, "and the Word was made flesh and dwelt among us" (Jn 1:14).

Here is also found the most compassionate sentence in the entire book of Revelation which extends to all the faithful, "God shall wipe away all tears from their eyes; and there shall be no more death, neither sorrow, nor crying, neither shall there be any more pain; for the former things have passed away" (v. 4).

God directly reveals: "I shall make all things new." This is established through God's fidelity and truthful assurance given to the faithful in this covenant. The words of God are confirmed by using, for the name of God, the Alpha and the Omega, the beginning and the end. Like the image of the shepherd, God leads the chosen and faithful ones to the life-giving waters.

Even more than the image of a flock with its shepherd is the stronger covenantal bonds of human and divine relationship — the faithful are sons and daughters of the living God (v. 7).

Almost as an aside there is a reminder that those who were faithless, cowardly, murderers, fornicators, idolaters, sorcerers, and liars are excluded for they have experienced the second death and have joined the devil in the burning sea of fire and sulfur. This is but a footnote in the splendid chapter describing the new creation in heaven and on earth. Notice that all of the crimes mentioned pertain to the commandments of God. We have seen in chapter 12 how such people, together with Satan and the beast, have persecuted and oppressed those who were the children of the woman and the witnesses to Jesus. It is her offspring who have kept the commandments and now experience the new creation.

The New Jerusalem (Rv 21:9-27)

The last of the seven angels who poured out the plagues now speaks to John and tells him to come and see the bride of the Lamb. What John is envisioning is the ideal of the Church universal living out the message to the seven churches with fidelity.

Like Habakkuk, the angel transports John in spirit to a high mountain and from that sacred setting, he sees the holy city Jerusalem descending from God and the heavens. We recall how mountains are the biblical location for encounter with God through prayer. Jesus prayed on the mountain; the Transfiguration took place on a mountain. Moses had the revelation of God's covenant and received the ten commandments on the mountain. Here the bride, the ideal image of the Church descends probably on Mount Zion, the stronghold of Jerusalem.

John describes the city as being constructed of the most precious of jewels, with golden streets so pure that they are almost as transparent as glass. The twelve tribes of Israel have their names inscribed on the gates of the perfectly symmetrical holy city and those of the twelve apostles of the Lamb (Jesus) are seen on the foundation stones of the city. God's covenant with Israel is shown in the twelve tribes while the covenant made with the Church is seen in the twelve apostles of Jesus. The ecclesiology of the seer is an integrated one; universality and continuity are part of the integration seen in the Church. All of this splendid sight reflects the glory of God (*kabod Adonai*) (vv. 11-14).

The Measuring of the Holy City (Rv 21:15)

From the allusions to the Hebrew Scriptures ever-present in the narrative, we can easily deduce that this section is based on the lengthy description of the measuring of the temple in 573 B.C.E. in a vision of the prophet Ezekiel. There is also a parallel in Zc 2:1-5. Both of these prophets are sources for John of Patmos.

Measurement shows preservation. Here it is done appropriately by an angel with a rod of gold. The measurements result in a symmetrical cube of fifteen hundred miles indicating the spaciousness of the heavenly Jerusalem. Then, in a overwhelming listing of precious stones, the narrator names twelve gems that are priceless. Neither the enumeration of Ex 28:17-21, nor of Is 53:11-12, or Ezk 16:9-13; 27:12-24 comes close to the enumeration given by the seer of Patmos. I personally found it fascinating to read the columns in the *Encyclopedia Brittanica* describing the color of these gems and telling where they are located. An excellent photo of them is available in the same encyclopedia. The beauty of the heavenly city is crowned with a giant pearl on each of its gates and the whole city glistens with a gold that is almost transparent. The vision is kaleidoscopic and mystical.

Finally, the visionary saw no temple in the realm of God for God is the Sacred Presence in need of no temple. Nor is there need for any created light whether of sun or moon. All is centered on the glory of God, the *Shekinah*, (the divine Presence) and the light emanating from the presence of the Lamb.

There is total freedom for those dwelling within the holy city. Nations and kings lend their glory to the city. All those who are written in the Book of Life belonging to the Lamb are citizens of the New Jerusalem. The idolaters and deceivers are excluded from this sacred dwelling place of God and the Lamb (v. 27).

Food for the Journey:

Isaiah 65:17-21

[17]For I am about to create new heavens and a new earth; the former things shall not be remembered or come to mind. [18]But be glad and rejoice forever in what I am creating; for I am about to create Jerusalem as a joy, and its people as a delight. [19]I will rejoice in Jerusalem, and delight in my people; no more shall the sound of weeping be heard in it, or the cry of distress. [20]No more shall there be in it an infant that lives but a few days, or an old person who does not live out a lifetime; for one who dies at a hundred years will be considered a youth, and one who falls short of a hundred will be considered accursed. [21]They shall build houses and inhabit them; they shall plant vineyards and eat their fruit.

Revelation 22:1-21

[1]Then the angel showed me the river of the water of life, bright as crystal, flowing from the throne of God and of the Lamb [2]through the middle of the street of the city. On either side of the river is the tree of life with its twelve kinds of fruit, producing its fruit each month; and the leaves of the tree are for the healing of the nations. [3]Nothing accursed will be found there any more. But the throne of God and of the Lamb will be in it, and his servants will worship him; [4]they will see his face, and his name will be on their foreheads. [5]And there will be no more night; they need no light of lamp or sun, for the Lord God will be their light, and they will reign forever and ever.

[6]And he said to me, "These words are trustworthy and true, for the Lord, the God of the spirits of the prophets, has sent his angel to show his servants what must soon take place." [7]"See, I am coming soon! Blessed is the one who keeps the words of the prophecy of this book." [8]I, John, am the one who heard and saw these things. And when I heard and saw them, I fell down to worship at the feet of the angel who showed them to me; [9]but he said to me, "You must not do that! I am a fellow servant with you

and your comrades the prophets, and with those who keep the words of this book. Worship God!"

¹⁰And he said to me, "Do not seal up the words of the prophecy of this book, for the time is near. ¹¹Let the evildoer still do evil, and the filthy still be filthy, and the righteous still do right, and the holy still be holy."

¹²"See, I am coming soon; my reward is with me, to repay according to everyone's work. ¹³I am the Alpha and the Omega, the first and the last, the beginning and the end."

¹⁴Blessed are those who wash their robes, so that they will have the right to the tree of life and may enter the city by the gates. ¹⁵Outside are the dogs and sorcerers and fornicators and murderers and idolaters, and everyone who loves and practices falsehood.

¹⁶"It is I, Jesus, who sent my angel to you with this testimony for the churches. I am the root and the descendant of David, the bright morning star."

¹⁷The Spirit and the bride say, "Come." And let everyone who hears say, "Come." And let everyone who is thirsty come. Let anyone who wishes take the water of life as a gift.

¹⁸I warn everyone who hears the words of the prophecy of this book: if anyone adds to them, God will add to that person the plagues described in this book; ¹⁹if anyone takes away from the words of the book of this prophecy, God will take away that person's share in the tree of life and in the holy city, which are described in this book. ²⁰The one who testifies to these things says, "Surely I am coming soon." Amen. Come, Lord Jesus! ²¹The grace of the Lord Jesus be with all the saints. Amen.

The Heavenly Vision Continues (Rv 22:1-5)

John's continuing vision is an experience similar to Ezekiel's vision of the water flowing from the eastern side of the temple (Ezk 47:1-2). There is also a river which has fruitful trees on both sides: "On the banks, on both sides of the river, there will grow all kinds of trees for food. Their leaves will not wither nor their fruit fail, but they will bear fresh fruit every month, because the water for them flows from the sanctuary." Their fruit will be for food, and their leaves for healing" (Ezk 47:12). Undoubtedly, this is a source for the author and seer in Revelation but there is also a difference. Ezekiel is speaking of the restoration of the earthly temple in Jerusalem while the mystic is now seeing the reality behind the veil taking place before the throne of God. Waters of life flow from the throne of God and the Lamb. The waters give life to the heavenly worshipers of God and the trees are yielding fruit as the months succeed each other; there is also healing (conversion achieved) in the leaves of the trees. There is both an earthly foundation for the vision and a heavenly one which transcends that of Ezekiel.

It is essential for John of Patmos to see the Lamb always associated with God and the throne of God. This is a high christology based on the paschal mystery of Jesus' death and resurrection. The victorious Christ is always central to the theology of Revelation. Both God and the Lamb are worshiped; the servants of God are attentive in action and in their praise to both God and the Lamb (v. 3).

No longer is there the fear of death when the faithful look upon the face of God for they have been signed with the name of the Lamb by their baptism and washed clean in his blood. We are close to Paul's theology of baptism: "Do you not know that all of us who have been baptized into Christ Jesus were baptized into his death? Therefore we have been buried with him by baptism into death, so that, just as Christ was raised from the dead by the glory of the Father, so we too might walk in the newness of life" (Rm 6:3-34).

The narrator then repeats what we have seen, namely, that there is no need for the light of lamp or sun, for God and the Lamb are the glorious light and lamp in heaven forever (see Rv 21:22-24).

John's mystical experience is coming to an end as the angel reminds him that all this is true and trustworthy and that these events will take place soon. This would be the Parousia or the Second Coming of the Lord. Jesus himself says, "See, I am coming soon! Blessed is the one who keeps the words of the prophecy of this book."

This passage has reversed the curse brought upon the human race in Gn 2:9: heaven is the new creation of the Garden of Eden and God is present among the worshipers and servants. Streams of life — eternal life — flow from the heavenly Mount Zion. God's promises made to the prophets are being fulfilled. There is great hope for the churches for all this is to happen soon.

Epilogue and Benediction (Rv 22:8-20)

We recall that every beginning is important in the Scriptures. The first chapter of Revelation is the prologue to John of Patmos' mystical visions and experience. Now he is directly listening to the angel of Revelation who speaks for Jesus. The commencement was a series of letters to the seven churches; now the epilogue is a summary that matches what the prologue contains. The parallels are self-evident as we approach the final prayer and benediction of Revelation.

John identifies himself just as he had in chapter one when he longed to celebrate the paschal mysteries in the Eucharist of the churches. His mystical experience through the angel of Revelation and through Jesus were, in a sense, such a celebration in his isolation on the island of Patmos. God gave him this special grace and called him to worship. The angel reminds him not to worship any human creature nor angelic being. The theme emerges once more as the vision ends and testimony is rendered to the truth of this prophetic book. "Worship God!" — a sure antidote for everything opposed to God and described in the three scrolls we have read or listened to.

Unlike other apocalyptic writings this one is not to be sealed. The Lamb has opened all seven seals; the same must be true for this sacred scroll from Patmos. "Do not seal up the words of the prophecy of this book, for the time is near" (v. 10).

Again we have a reminder that life on earth continues with

those doing evil opposed by those who do what is righteous; those continuing in immorality contrasted with the saints. There is still time for conversion seems to be the meaning of this text, but the time is short.

Jesus and God are identified in the same honorific and mysterious title: "I am the Alpha and the Omega, the first and the last, the beginning and the end" (v. 13). God is not an unknown power or force; God is not a cause or an absolute principle. God and Jesus are persons who extend the realm of heaven to those who are faithful witnesses and devout worshipers.

The seventh and last beatitude is aptly reserved for the epilogue. We are truly blessed because of the Baptism and Eucharist we share in the water and blood that flows from the throne and from the Lamb. Baptism and Eucharist are part of the spiritual life of the seven churches. Baptism enables the faithful to sacrifice their lives for the sake of God's Word (the Gospel). Jesus, in the Eucharist, has given his own life for the ransom of many. Jesus is the Paschal Lamb of the second testament.

In verse 16 Jesus speaks to the communities assuring them he is the suffering-servant Messiah. He is a true descendant of David and the bright morning star. The star of morning was considered divine. The star also is a second testament rereading of Nb 24:17: "A star shall come forth out of Jacob, and a scepter shall rise out of Israel." This reinforces the messianic claim for Jesus in the believing community.

As we end the Book of Revelation the narrator places us in an atmosphere of prayer that unites us to the seven churches. We are part of the mystery of the communion of saints. D.J. Harrington has reconstructed the verses in a liturgical response:

> And the Spirit of Jesus and the Bride say: "Come."
> And let anyone who hears say: "Come."
> And let one who thirsts: "Come."
> Whoever wills: "Take the Water of life, freely."
> (*Revelation: Sacra Pagina 16,*
> Glazier, Collegeville, MN, 1993, p. 223).

I am convinced that the prophecy of this book was to be read in the churches of Asia Minor during a liturgical celebration. The last prayer we have from the liturgy is repeated three times, showing the intensity of response that the believers are called to chant; Jesus has said, "Surely I am coming soon." The Communion of Saints (those who were, those who are, those who are yet to be) sing out, "Amen! Come, Lord Jesus! *Maranatha!*"

Food for the Journey:

Hymn Te Deum

> You are God: we praise you;
> You are the Lord; we acclaim you;
> You are the eternal Father:
> All creation worships you.
> To you all angels, all the powers of heaven,
> Cherubim and Seraphim, sing in endless praise:
> Holy, holy, holy, Lord, God of power and might,
> heaven and earth are full of your glory.
> The glorious company of apostles praise you.
> The noble fellowship of prophets praise you.
> The white-robed army of martyrs praise you.
> Throughout the world the holy church acclaims you:
> Father, of majesty unbounded,
> your true and only Son, worthy of all worship,
> and the Holy Spirit, advocate and guide.
> You, Christ, are the king of glory,
> the eternal Son of the Father.
> When you became man to set us free
> you did not spurn the Virgin's womb.
> You overcame the sting of death,
> and opened the kingdom of heaven to all believers.
> You are seated at God's right hand in glory.
> We believe that you will come, and be our judge.
> Come then, Lord, and help your people,
> bought with the price of your own blood,
> and bring us with your saints
> to glory everlasting.

GLOSSARY FOR THE BOOK OF REVELATION

ALPHA: The first letter of the Greek alphabet. It is used to show the eternity of God or of Jesus, the Lamb in Revelation. It is accompanied by the last letter of the alphabet, Omega in order to show that God is both the beginning and the end of all creation.

APOCALYPTIC: This is a literary form of communication which emphasizes the end times. It is given in symbolic and dramatic fashion in the book of Revelation. Daniel is also an apocalyptic writing in the Hebrew Scriptures. Also see the "little apocalypse" of Mark, chapter 13.

APOCALYPSE: The first word used in the book of Revelation. It means to uncover, to unveil, or to reveal. Both Apocalypse and Revelation are used as the title for the last book of the New Testament.

ARMAGEDDON: The place where the rulers and kings of the earth will gather for the final battle of good versus evil. It is symbolic in Revelation. Some scholars think it is Megiddo, the most famous battlefield of ancient Israel.

BEATITUDE: A declaration of blessedness on a person or community for its fidelity in virtue. It is also good fortune, reward, and happiness. There are seven beatitudes or *macarisms* in the book of Revelation. There are 57 beatitudes in the Hebrew Scriptures including the deutero-canonical works.

CANONICAL: This word is taken from the Greek word *kanon* which means a rule or guiding principle. The list of the New Testament books as a standard.

CHRISTOLOGY: This is literally the "study of Christ" or the titles and names given to Jesus in the New Testament, for example, *Son of Man, Son of God, Word, Savior*. The word itself is taken from *Christos* which means the *anointed one* or the *Messiah*.

DISPENSATIONALISM: A system for interpreting the Bible invented by John Nelson Darby (1800-1882). It affirms that God dealt with people through seven dispensations or eras. The seven are (1) innocence, (2) conscience, (3) human government, (4) promise, (5) law, (6) church, (7) kingdom. Dispensationalists look at chapter 20 of Revelation very literally.

ECCLESIOLOGY: This is the study of the Church (*ekklesia, ecclesia* in Greek and Latin). Any passage that refers to the assembly of Christians or the community belongs to this category of theology. The book of Revelation contains a message for the seven churches of Asia Minor.

ESCHATOLOGY: This is the study of the last things to happen in the world and the cosmos. It may be termed imminent and urgent such as we have in Revelation and Mark 13. It is also termed realized eschatology in John and Luke. The Second Coming of Christ or the Parousia is considered to be an eschatological term. So, too, in Catholic thought, heaven, hell, purgatory, and judgment belong to this category.

GOG: This is a cryptic name given in Rv 20:8. The name is borrowed from Ezk, cc. 38-39. Gog is permitted to attack the kingdom of God after the 1000 years during which Satan is bound. Historically, this may refer to King Gyges of Lydia (650 B.C.E.). In Rv 20:8, Magog, which was a geographical place, becomes another cryptic name with Gog.

KOINE: The word means common; in the New Testament it is the name given to the common Greek used in writing and speaking during the time of the formation of the New Testament.

KOINONIA: The close fellowship or partnership shared by the communities in the New Testament. It can also mean partnership, contribution, or gift. It symbolizes the mutual love and respect that Church members have for each other.

MACARISM: This is the Greek expression for a beatitude, hence, good fortune, blessing, happiness in a faithful person.

MARIOLOGY: This is the theology or study of Mary in the New Testament and in Catholic Tradition. It is important to relate anything said about Mary to Christology and Ecclesiology. It comes under consideration in chapter 12 of Revelation where there may be a secondary interpretation of the *Woman* as Mary. Primarily, the *Woman* is the Church.

MILLENNIALISM: In Revelation this pertains to the 1000 years mentioned in chapter 20. Some believe that Christ will reign on this earth for a thousand years before the end-time comes. A period of great happiness, good government, and freedom from wickedness for God's people.

MYTH: In biblical studies this is a positive word used to describe what is transcendent yet comes into our world. It is an attempt to talk about the divine in terms more appropriate to our human activity. It is also a strong motivational foundational story which influences our behavior. It is a sacred narrative.

NARRATIVE: The telling of the story in a literary form. In biblical studies, narrative criticism does not theologize or historicize the text. The narrator, the implied and intended readers, the real author and the real world are included in this biblical approach.

NUMBERS: Both in the Hebrew Scriptures and in the New Testament certain numbers have a symbolic meaning. Since the book of Revelation alludes to many passages from the Hebrew Scriptures it uses certain numbers. Seven is the symbol for completeness. Twelve is also a sacred number of completeness: the tribes of Israel are twelve; Jesus has 12 apostles; twelve stars surround the head of the woman in chapter 12. The number 3 shares in the perfection of 7. It is used 31 times in Revelation. Four shares in the perfection of 7. It is used 20 times in Revelation. 1000 and all numbers with zeroes indicate an unlimited number. The famous 666 in Revelation is a bad number and signifies absolute incompleteness. 1260 is the same as the three and one half years or days that are mentioned in revelation. Twenty-four is a positive number, probably referring both to the 12 tribes of Israel and the 12 apostles.

OMEGA: The last letter of the Greek alphabet. In Revelation it is used to designate God or Jesus as the end or goal of all creation. It is used with the Alpha or first letter in Greek which shows that God is the beginning of all creation.

PANTOCRATOR: In Revelation this term refers to God seen as the *Almighty One*. In Greek culture it is the great image of Christ, a painting or mosaic which is often to be found in the cupola or area above the altar. The image tends to be overwhelming in these sanctuaries and captures in art the sense of God or Jesus as the Lord of the cosmos.

PROPHECY: This is derived from the Greek word which almost always denotes one who communicates divine revelation. John of Patmos, the author of Revelation, is called to be a prophet. He is to speak or present his message before others. It is helpful to situate prophecy not as a prediction of future events; rather it is a message from God dealing with situations that demand a response. It usually involves issues of social justice and correct judgment.

RAPTURE: This term is not used anywhere in the Greek Bible. It is used by certain biblical fundamentalists who believe that the *Rapture* will occur for the Church when Satan is loosed after the 1000 years as mentioned in Rv 20:7. This idea became popular only in the nineteenth century.

REDACTION: This refers to the editorial work that has been done on a writing. Perhaps John of Patmos redacted several Jewish writings and put them into his own composition. Redaction Criticism is a method in New Testament and Hebrew Testament studies in which the theological intention of an author of a biblical text is clarified. It takes note of the literary techniques, emendations, and themes that are threaded throughout the biblical composition.

SOTERIOLOGY: The word comes from the Greek *Soter* which means savior. Soteriology is the study of the saving action of Jesus Christ in the mystery of his death on the Cross. The Passion, Death, and Resurrection pertain to the soteriology of the New Testament. In Revelation this idea may be one of the key concepts behind the writing of Revelation for the book shows that the Christ is ultimately victorious over death, sin, and Satan (Evil personified).

SYMBOLISM: This refers to the overall effect or use of symbols within a literary piece. The word itself means to compare or to bring together. Usually it refers to a literary or philological sign or number which has a hidden meaning. Some religious symbols help the believer to have access to the spiritual or supernatural. Symbolism is at its peak in such writings as Ezekiel, Daniel, Zechariah, and the book of Revelation.

WORLDS OF THE TEXT: There are four worlds for the literary observation of texts whether biblical texts or otherwise. These worlds are helpful for understanding the point of view and methodology used by a scholar when he or she examines the texts. The worlds are:

1. The world *behind* the text: In the study of biblical works, this is also called exegesis, that is, an interpretation based on the best critical text; it is scientific and objective. Exegesis enables the reader to know what the text meant in its original formulation by the writer. Historical criticism, philology (study of the words in the original language), social location, and the intention of the author or redactor (editor) are included in this world behind the text. Barr writes, "The great strength of this historical method in all areas of study has been to free us from the tyranny of our present situation by showing us the past."

2. The world *within* the text: Revelation as literature constructed with all of the different patterns and structures of the language used are the object of this world or interpretative method. For example, most Gospels are in narrative form. There are within this world such literary techniques as parables, metaphors, and paradoxes. There is poetry and prose. Literary genres are detected; styles are evident. A study of this world involves determining *how* the text is put together or its rhetoric. The writer's ethos or point of view is also observed. For example, in Revelation the ethos or point of view of the prophet is that we should "Worship only God!" The emotions of the visionary show us his pathos; finally, his concentric story telling is his logos, the order and reasoning he uses in his story.

3. The world *in front* of the text: This refers to the way the text is read in light of our contemporary culture and the challenges we face when reading the text. We are always influenced by our own culture and background when reading the New Testament. There is also the long history of many interpretations of a text and we know some of them or buy into them. Readers and theologians, scholars and pastors read and interpret the text in the light of today's problems. We critique our own society or that of the biblical text when reading in this world of the text. There is always the need to make the text relevant to our time and to our own concerns. This makes this world in front of the text so important. The above two worlds are necessary in order to make this world of the text an effective one.

4. The world of *the text itself*: The book of Revelation is available to anyone who reads it. A skeptic, a believer, a searcher is able to read this book and understand what they can of it or give it a completely new meaning. Even cartoonists are able to make use of the book of Revelation. Barr writes, "The New Critics, as they call themselves, argued that works of literature are autonomous and independent: once an author sends a poem out into the world the author loses all control over it. The whole meaning of the poem is found in the poem, according to these critics."

SELECTED BIBLIOGRAPHY

Aune, D.E., *Revelation: Word Biblical Commentary*, Vol. 52A, Dallas, Texas, Word Books.

_____, *Revelation 6-16*, Vol. 52B. Nashville, T. Nelson, 1998.

_____, *Revelation 17-22*, Vol. 52C, Nashville, T. Nelson, 1998.

Barr, D.L., *Tales of the End: A Narrative Commentary of the Book of Revelation*, Santa Rosa, CA: Polebridge Press, 1998.

_____, *An Introduction: New Testament Story*, NY: Wadsworth (1995), 377-418.

Branick, V.P., *Understanding the New Testament: An Introduction*, NY: Paulist Press (1998), 356-376.

Brown, R.E., Donfried, K.P., Fitzmyer, J.A., Reumann, J., *Mary in the New Testament*, Philadelphia, PA (1978), 219-239.

Brown, R.E., *An Introduction to the New Testament*. New York: Doubleday (1997), 773-813.

Brown, R.E., Fitzmyer, J.A., Murphy, R.E., eds. *The Jerome Biblical Commentary*, Englewood Cliffs, NJ: Prentice (1968); *The Apocalypse*, D'Aragon, J.L., 64:467-498.

_____, eds. *The New Jerome Biblical Commentary*, Englewood Cliffs, NJ: Prentice (1990): *The Apocalypse (Revelation)*, Collins, A. Yarbro, 63:996-1016.

Buby, B.A., *Mary of Galilee: Mary in the New Testament*, Staten Island, NY: Alba House (1994), 141-164.

Collins, A. Yarbro, *Crisis and Catharsis: The Power of the Apocalypse*, Philadelphia, PA: Westminster, 1984.

Corsini, E., *The Apocalypse: The Perennial Revelation of Jesus*

Christ, trans. & ed. Moloneyor, F.J., Good News Studies, 5, Wilmington, DE: Glazier, 1983.

Ford, Massyingberde, J., *Revelation: A New Translation with Introduction and Commentary*, Anchor Bible, 38, NY: Doubleday, 1975.

Fuller, R.C., Johnson, L., Kearns, C., eds., *A New Catholic Commentary on Holy Scripture Revelation (The Apocalypse)*, Scullion, J., NY: Thomas Nelson (rev. 1975), 1266-1283.

Harrington, W.J., *Revelation: Sacra Pagina 16*, Collegeville, MN: Glazier, 1993.

Harper Collins, *Study Bible: New Revised Standard Version*, NY: Harper Collins, *The Revelation to John (Apocalypse)*, Aune, D. (1993): 2307-2337.

Kealy, S. J., *The Apocalypse of John: Message of Biblical Spirituality*, Vol. 15, Wilmington, DE: Glazier, 1987.

Léon-Dufour, X., *Dictionary of the New Testament*, San Francisco: Harper & Row, 1980.

Newsom, C.A., Ringe, S.H., *The Women's Bible Commentary*, Revelation (Susan Garrett), Louisville, KY: Westminster/Know (1992), 377-382.

de la Potterie, Ignace, S.J., *Mary in the Mystery of the Covenant*, Staten Island, NY: Alba House (1992), 239- 266.

Schüssler, Fiorenza, E., *Revelation: Vision of A Just World*, Minneapolis, MN: Fortress, 1991.

Sena, P.J., *The Apocalypse: Biblical Revelation Explained*, Staten Island, NY: Alba House, 1983.